Deeper Christian Faith

REVISED EDITION

Ted Campbell

All Saints Day, 2019

Deeper Christian Faith

REVISED EDITION

A Re-Sounding

BY

Ted A. Campbell

Foreword by George A. Mason

CASCADE *Books* · Eugene, Oregon

DEEPER CHRISTIAN FAITH, REVISED EDITION
A Re-Sounding

Cascade Books
An Imprint of Wipf and Stock Publishers
199 W. 8th Ave., Suite 3
Eugene, OR 97401

www.wipfandstock.com

PAPERBACK ISBN: 978-1-5326-5752-8
HARDCOVER ISBN: 978-1-5326-5753-5
EBOOK ISBN: 978-1-5326-5754-2

Cataloguing-in-Publication data:

Names: Campbell, Ted, author. | Mason, George A., foreword.

Title: Deeper Christian faith : a re-sounding / Ted A. Campbell ; foreword by George A. Mason.

Description: Eugene, OR : Cascade Books, 2019. | Includes bibliographical references and index.

Identifiers: ISBN 978-1-5326-5752-8 (paperback) | ISBN 978-1-5326-5753-5 (hardcover) | ISBN 978-1-5326-5754-2 (ebook)

Subjects: LCSH: Christianity—21st century.| Theology, Doctrinal—History—21st century. | Faith. | Apologetics—History—21st century.

Classification: BR121.3 .C36 2019 (paperback) | BR121.3 .C36 (ebook)

Manufactured in the U.S.A.   09/11/19

For further information and resources on *Deeper Christian Faith*: http://deeperchristianfaith.org

to

Elizabeth Marie

*And it came to pass
that when Elisabeth
heard the salutation of Mary . . .*
—LUKE 1:41 (KJV)

Contents

Foreword

by George A. Mason
Wilshire Baptist Church, Dallas, Texas

IT'S NEVER A COMPLIMENT when someone is said to be "a mile wide and an inch deep." No matter how valuable a person's breadth of knowledge or interests, depth adds heft. This is especially true in the spiritual realm.

"Putting on Christ," as Saint Paul describes the process of faith being formed as a Christian (Gal 3:27), is a lifelong practice for followers of Jesus.[1] We are baptized into participation in the life of God. Well-worn habits of heart, head, and hands then clothe us with virtues that characterize us as children of God.

The essence of what the church calls catechesis is just one generation handing on to the next the faith once received. When the faith handed on is received over and over again, the life of Christ increasingly shines forth in a person, revealing the true self God always intended. This is the abundant life Jesus promised (John 10:10). This is "the life that really is life" (1 Tim 6:19).

Ted A. Campbell has given us a way to dive deeper into the faith. In this volume, *A Deeper Christian Faith*, he invites us to join those who have gone before us and left us paths of wisdom that combine knowledge and love. He takes us to the center of what it means to be a Christian.

The church has a long history of writing catechisms to instruct new converts in the faith and to strengthen the faith of those who want to go deeper. Over the centuries, these catechisms have been attached to different branches of the church—whether Catholic, Orthodox, Lutheran, Reformed, nondenominational, or other denominational. Campbell's ecumenical spirit calls the church back together around the work of forming faith in which the whole church—including all members, whether young

1. Unless otherwise noted, all Scripture citations in this book are from the New Revised Standard Version (NRSV).

or old, new or seasoned followers—and the church as a whole—regardless of denomination—engages.

As a Baptist pastor and theologian, I appreciate the inclusive nature of this work. We Baptists practice Christian baptism by immersion, partly because we believe it to be a vivid depiction of the life we enter by faith. But whether your tradition immerses or sprinkles or pours, the call to faith is always a call to dive in. We can't tiptoe around in the shallows and expect to experience a meaningful Christian life. We must wade into the deep, letting go of our instinct to preserve ourselves at all cost. And when we do, something miraculous, surprising and beautiful happens: we feel the buoyant gift of new life that comes from the same Spirit that raised Jesus from the dead.

Faith is a way of looking at the world that includes what we cannot see, and yet believe is as real as what we can see. It begins with knowing God and continues by learning to trust in the goodness of God and the promise of salvation in Jesus Christ. The initiating ritual of baptism shapes our identity in Christ, and the Lord's Supper feeds us at the table with our family of faith. Time-honored disciplines of the Christian faith allow the Spirit of God to work in us, on us, and for us as a life of holy love emerges.

This book is for beginners and for beginners-again, those who are fresh to the faith and those who need a refresher in the faith. Whether read devotionally or studied in a group, *A Deeper Christian Faith* will deepen your Christian faith.

No one wants to be a spiritual lightweight. A weightier soul awaits on the other side of entering deeper into the Christian faith as known and practiced by those who have come before us. Think of *A Deeper Christian Faith* as a spiritual weight trainer that promises a fitter faith when read and practiced.

An effective catechism leads us faithfully along the holy path that brings us at last into the fullness of God's presence. By walking the way of Christ with saints of every age, we are transformed: stronger and deeper at the end than at the beginning. The poet Charles Wesley concluded his beautiful hymn "Love Divine, All Loves Excelling" with these words:

> Changed from glory into glory,
> till in heaven we take our place,
> till we cast our crowns before thee,
> lost in wonder, love, and praise.[2]

---

2. Charles Wesley, hymn "Jesus, Shew Us Thy Salvation," originally published in *Hymns for Those that Seek*, 13–14; adapted as the hymn "Love Divine, All Loves Excelling," here as given in United Methodist Church, *United Methodist Hymnal*, no. 384.

Author's Preface

ΠΑΡΕΔωΚΑ ΓΑΡ ΥΜΙΝ
ΕΝ ΠΡωΤΟΙΟ
Ο ΚΑΙ ΠΑΡΕΛΛΒΟΝ

FOR I HANDED ON TO YOU
AS OF FIRST IMPORTANCE
WHAT I ALSO RECEIVED

—1 Corinthians 15:3[1]

THE PURPOSE OF *Deeper Christian Faith* is to form Christians in such a depth of Christian faith, grounded in biblical, historical, and ecumenical insights, that they can state with confidence what they believe and practice in common with other Christians and grow in the life of self-giving love at the heart of the Christian faith.

I have called *Deeper Christian Faith* **a "re-sounding."** This expression is derived from the root word of *catechesis* and *catechism*, words used in early Christian centuries for basic instruction in the Christian faith. The root word means "to sound down" into the ears of hearers (see chapter 3). But *Deeper Christian Faith* is a "re-sounding," **a re-catechism**. It offers a deeper form of training in Christian faith for those who were catechized early in life and stand in need of richer, renewed formation, or perhaps for adult Christians who have not been formed deeply in historic Christian beliefs and practices.[2]

1. Excerpts from the Greek New Testament have been checked against Jongkind et al., *Greek New Testament*, s.v. in each case. The New Testament translations are usually my own, in which I try to give a very literal translation remaining close to the original text and following the division of lines, as in the Greek text shown.

2. I am grateful to Cascade Books editor Charlie M. Collier for suggesting the subtitle

The English word "sounding" also suggests **depth**, as a poet has expressed it using the nautical metaphor of "sounding" depths:

> In vain the first-born seraph tries
> to sound the depths of Love Divine
>
> (Charles Wesley, 1739).[3]

This book is designed to convey depth. It is not trying to "make" Christian teachings "relevant" to the contemporary world as if they weren't. Quite the opposite. This is to enable contemporary readers to experience the rich, alien, and mysterious worlds of historic Christian teachings and practices, an ocean of exquisite intricacies spanning cultures and languages from ancient times to the present.[4] "Put out into the deep water" (Luke 5:4).

If I had to describe my approach in this book, I might call it **neo-primitivist**. But this does not mean an attempt to replicate an idealized moment from the past. Modern historians aren't allowed to idealize the past. For me, it means an attempt to clear out some of the clutter and pretense that so often obscures what has been historically central to Christian communities. It involves a quest for simplicity and clarity, a retreat from disarray towards a place from which we can see what has been centrally important to Christian communities since the earliest times. It might mean that I am hopelessly Protestant despite all my catholic proclivities. I have Campbell family roots in the radically primitivist Churches of Christ. But primitivist movements arose long before Protestants. The earliest Christian monks had a primitivist vision for Christian faith, as did Saint Francis of Assisi and the Franciscan movement he fostered. And this vision is **neo**: it is for now. The world in which I live and the churches in which I minister today desperately need some primitive simplicity and clarity.[5]

"A Re-Sounding."

3. See Charles Wesley's poem "Free Grace" in the 1739 edition of Wesley and Wesley, *Hymns and Sacred Poems*, 118.

4. The font utilized for the English translations of focus texts is GFS Nicefore. The font utilized in Latin and Greek focus texts is GFS Jackson. Both of these fonts replicate scripts used in early Christian Greek manuscripts. Both were designed by George D. Matthiopoulos and have been made available through the Greek Font Society. These fonts have been released through a FreeFont license; see the website of the Greek Font Society at http://www.greekfontsociety.gr.

5. I intend the term "neo-primitivist" to stand beside other kindred Christian movements for bringing modernities and tradition into direct dialogue, such as Neo-Orthodoxy or the "paleo-orthodox" vision of Christian faith that Thomas C. Oden first enunciated (though not with that term) in his *Agenda for Theology*. I have also been

I hope that my work as a historian, my exposure to other Christian traditions than my own, and my participation in formal ecumenical dialogues give me grounds for responsibly enunciating such a vision. *A Deeper Christian Faith* focuses on what I have studied and know—namely, the historical and ecumenical grounds for common (shared) Christian teachings and practices. Its seven chapters focus on historic Christian faith as affirmed together by Christian communities in the last hundred years.[6]

A Deeper Christian Faith is indebted to a number of other forms of catechesis (catechisms) and single-volume accounts of Christian beliefs and practices that have influenced this book, including C. S. Lewis's *Mere Christianity*.[7] A very recent and remarkable publication is *Christianity: Fundamental Teachings*, produced by the Joint Commission of Churches in Turkey, reflecting agreements between Eastern Orthodox, Oriental Orthodox, Catholic, and Protestant church bodies in Turkey, a work that brings a very distinctive perspective on common Christian teachings and practices from the minority Christian churches in the area that in ancient times was called Asia Minor.[8]

The book is dedicated to our daughter Elizabeth Marie. At her confirmation, she engaged in a small act of youthful rebellion by remaining silent in response to a question that asked if she would be loyal to a particular Christian denomination. That was her way of valuing what is commonly Christian, and that is what this book is about.[9]

influenced by the approach to modernity in the Conservative movement in Judaism, and especially by its focus on religious practices.

6. I have had reference to key ecumenical consensus documents, including the following consistently used documents: 1) the World Council of Churches Faith and Order Commission's consensus document, *Baptism, Eucharist and Ministry*; 2) their study *Confessing the One Faith: An Ecumenical Explication of the Apostolic Faith as it is Confessed in the Nicene-Constantinopolitan Creed (381)*; 3) the "Joint Declaration on the Doctrine of Justification" affirmed by the Catholic Church and the Lutheran World Federation in 1999 and subsequently affirmed (2006) by the World Methodist Council (in Pelikan and Hotchkiss, *Creeds and Confessions of Faith*, 3:877–88).

7. Lewis, *Mere Christianity*. Some other single-volume works include Bilezikian, *Christianity 101*; Ratzinger, *Introduction to Christianity*; Harkness, *What Christians Believe*; Barth, *Dogmatics in Outline*; Hordern, *Layman's Guide*.

8. Joint Commission of Churches in Turkey, *Christianity: Fundamental Teachings*.

9. I express my gratitude to a number of persons who have helped with this project. In writing the first edition of this book, I utilized an advisory group consisting of Rev. Eradio Valverde (United Methodist Church); Brother Jeffrey Gros, FSC, of blessed memory (Catholic Church); Rev. Barbara Kenley (Presbyterian Church in the USA); Dr. Todd Von Helms (Southern Baptist Church); Rev. Kathleene Card (United Methodist

Author's Preface

Church); and Dr. John T. Ford, CSC (Catholic University of America). Dr. Carole Monica Burnett also read the entire manuscript from her unique perspective as a Catholic Christian who later became Antiochian Orthodox. Similarly, Dr. W. Hall Harris (Dallas Theological Seminary) offered comments from the perspective of a contemporary New Testament scholar and from the perspective of conservative evangelical churches on both the first and second editions of the book.

Ritual of Handing on the Faith

Presider:
    I handed on to you as of first importance
    what I in turn had received:

Community:
    that Christ died for our sins
    in accordance with the scriptures,
    and that he was buried,
    and that he was raised on the third day
    in accordance with the scriptures.

All (said or sung, repeated if desired):
    Thy word is a lamp unto my feet
    and a light unto my path.

Notes on the Ritual of Handing on the Faith

The initial text is the NRSV translation of 1 Corinthians 15:3–4, reflecting the words by which Saint Paul received and transmitted the Christian message. The concluding verse reflects the KJV (AV) translation of Psalm 119:105.

The ritual can be used at the beginning and the conclusion of sessions for *Deeper Christian Faith*. At the beginning of the session, a presider may hold a lighting candle and use it to light a fixed candle (or oil-burning lamp) during the community's response. The presider extinguishes the lighting candle after the fixed candle is lit.

At the conclusion of a session, the presider may hold the unlit lighting candle, light it from the fixed candle, and then extinguish the fixed candle during the community's response.

Another idea would be to use an oil-burning lamp in place of a candle that will remain fixed and lit in the front of the assembly during the session. It is important that either a candle or oil-burning lamp should be used; they will serve as an illustration of the phrase "light from light" in the Nicene Creed, and electric lights will not convey the sense of this phrase, i.e., one light that is derived from another light.

If a congregation has a permanent (perpetual) lamp, the lighting candle might be lit from it as a sign of continuity in the handing-on of the faith.

The fixed candle (or lamp) might be placed in front of a cross or a Christ icon.

A suggested tune for the Psalm verse is that of Michael W. Smith. Host communities should be sure that they have appropriate license to use this and any other musical resources.

CHAPTER 1

Holy God

Naming an Unknown God

I WANT TO INVITE you to a deeper Christian faith. Look right through this screen into an ancient world. If you're looking at paper instead of a screen, then you're slightly closer to the ancient world, but in either case, look at the text below to see a sentence delivered in the first century AD by the apostle Paul. Paul was upset by the religious objects he had seen in Athens. Speaking in Greek on Mars Hill, here's what he said, according to an ancient text called *Praxeis Apostolōn* or the Acts of the Apostles:

ΔΙΕΡΧΟΜΕΝΟC ΓΑΡ ΚΑΙ ΑΝΑΘΕωΡωΝ
ΤΑ CΕΒΑCΜΑΤΑ ΥΜωΝ
ΕΥΡΟΝ ΚΑΙ ΒωΜΟΝ ΕΝ ω ΕΠΕΓΕΓΡΑΠΤΟ
ΑΓΝωCΤω ΘΕω

FOR GOING ABOUT AND LOOKING AT
THE OBJECTS OF YOUR WORSHIP
I ALSO FOUND ONE ALTAR INSCRIBED
TO AN UNKNOWN GOD

—Acts 17:23

The apostle Paul could have taken a different approach. He could have walked through Athens screaming bloody murder and denouncing all the

1

religious shrines he found as sinister objects of evil deities. But somehow the apostle found a bit more compassion for the Athenians when he spoke on Mars Hill. **His speech suggested that the Athenians—some of them, at least—were worshiping the one God as "an unknown God."** He then proceeded to reveal this "unknown God" to them.

In their work of sharing the "good news" (gospel), Christian communities have sometimes followed Paul's insight in claiming that the God Christians worship is the same God that other people have worshiped.[1] Christians after the New Testament period would have little trouble identifying Plato's belief in one God as a precursor of Christian beliefs.

But there are limits to this liberality. Christian communities have insisted that there can be none but one God.[2] Historic Christian communities concur with the central Jewish affirmation called the *Shema*. Look once again into a distant and ancient world. This affirmation appears in the Hebrew language in an ancient book called *Devarim* or Deuteronomy:

שמע ישראל יהוה אלהינו יהוה אחד

HEAR O ISRAEL

יהוה IS OUR GOD

יהוה ALONE

—Deuteronomy 6:4[3]

Something weird is going on here, indicated by **a mysterious name of God** that appears twice in this passage. The name יהוה has four consonants that are roughly Y-H-W-H. Traditional Jewish communities consider this name to be so sacred that they do not pronounce it, and biblical texts do

---

1. By utilizing the Hebrew and Aramaic Scriptures that Christians call the Old Testament, proto-orthodox Christian communities affirmed continuity with the God of Israel. As we shall see in chapter 2, the earliest versions of the Christian message (e.g., 1 Corinthians 15:1–4) maintained that the central elements of the Christian message were "according to the [Jewish] scriptures" (World Council of Churches Faith and Order Commission, *Confessing the One Faith*, ¶¶ 31–35).

2. World Council of Churches Faith and Order Commission, *Confessing the One Faith*, ¶¶ 6–35.

3. I have checked Old Testament excerpts against Kittel, *Biblia Hebraica* [*Biblia Hebraica Stuttgartensia*]. In most cases, the translation is that of the New Revised Standard Version, as in this case, except substituting the Hebrew letters of the four-letter name of God for the circumlocution "the Lord."

not give vowels for it. In its place, Jewish communities pronounce a word, *Adonai*, that means "the Lord."

In fact, older English translations of the Bible indicated this weirdness by putting the word "Lᴏʀᴅ" in place of this name. The King James Version of the Bible sometimes used a strange, made-up word "Jehovah" in place of this name that combined the four consonants for this word with the vowels for the word *Adonai*. That's even weirder. Some biblical scholars have hypothesized that the name might have been pronounced more like "Yahweh," but **there is no tradition of pronunciation for this word, so nobody really knows how it was pronounced**. If you want to see it written out as a word you can try pronouncing, you're out of luck here. When you see יהוה in this book, it represents the unpronounced divine name. You can say "Lord" or "the Lord" or (following the Jewish custom) *Adonai* or perhaps *Ha Shem* ("the name") at those points.

The *Shema* asserts that the God whom Israel worships as יהוה and as "our God" is, in fact, **the one and only God**; only יהוה is God. This claim about the oneness or unity of God is a fundamental belief of Jewish communities and a belief that Christian groups consistently follow. Early Christians expressed this conviction by utilizing a common dialect of the Greek language as their principal means of communication. Embedded throughout the New Testament is a Greek phrase, *o theos*,[4] that literally means "the god," but which we translate "God" with the capital letter "G," indicating belief in one God.[5]

This could have some scary political implications. If God is the one Lord, then Christian and Jewish communities can't acknowledge Cyrus of Persia as the Lord, they can't acknowledge Caesar of Rome as the Lord, and they can't acknowledge a Führer as the Lord. You can continue this list right up to your own time and place. **Jews and Christians would give up their lives rather than acknowledge any other lord in place of the Lord.**

Belief in one God has not been limited to Christian and Jewish communities. The founders of **Islam** were familiar with Judaism and Christianity. The *Shahādah*, the principal affirmation of Muslims, begins with the claim "There is no god except God." You'll sometimes see this translated as "There is no god but Allāh," but it is important to realize that *Allāh* is the common

4. In transliterating Greek words, I have left off the letter "h" representing the rough breathing mark at the beginning of words in deference to the fact that the breathing marks were not part of the early textual tradition and the fact that they are not pronounced in the tradition of Greek churches.

5. Kittel and Friedrich, *Theological Dictionary of the New Testament*, 3:65–119, s.v. "θεός"; esp. 90, "ὁ θεός refers to the one God of Israel."

noun meaning "God" used by Jews and Christians as well as Muslims who speak the Arabic language. The intention of the Qur'ān, the *Shahādah*, and the Muslim religious tradition more broadly, was to claim that the one God Muslims worship is the same God whom Jews and Christians worship,[6] just as the intention of Christian communities has been to claim that the God Christians worship is the same God whom Jews worship.[7]

A "Very Good" Material World

Along with the affirmation of the oneness of God, Christian communities also want to affirm with Jews that the one God is the maker of the material world, and that it is God's good creation.[8] The Bible begins with this affirmation in the ancient book of *Bereshit* or Genesis:

בראשית ברא אלהים
את השמים ואת הארץ

IN THE BEGINNING GOD CREATED
THE HEAVENS AND THE EARTH

—Genesis 1:1[9]

6. The *Shahādah* is cited as given in Ayoub, *Islam*, 55; see also 51–52 for Ayoub's discussion of *Allāh* as the common word for God used by Arabic-speaking Jews, Christians, and Muslims. The Joint Commission of Churches in Turkey points out that in Turkey, Christians refer to Jesus Christ as "the Word of Allah" and as "the Spirit of Allah" (*Christianity*, 20). For contemporary perspectives on the question of whether Christians, Jews, and Muslims worship "the same God," see Neusner et al., *Jews, Christians, and Muslims*. I do not mean to offer simple or easy answers to this question, and my comments here claim only that it is the *intention* of Christianity and Islam to worship the same God as Jews worship; it does not pass judgment on the much larger question of whether Christians, Jews, and Muslims do in fact worship precisely "the same God."

7. Writing in the context of contemporary Muslim-majority Turkey, the Joint Commission of Churches in Turkey publication *Christianity: Fundamental Teachings* begins with the claim that "Christianity is a monotheistic religion" (13); see the section "We Believe in One God" (26–27).

8. World Council of Churches Faith and Order Commission, *Confessing the One Faith*, ¶¶ 63–89.

9. The translation here conforms to that of the NRSV, though omitting the word "when" that the NRSV used to connect the next phrase.

4

The most universal of Christian creeds, the Nicene Creed of the fourth century AD, begins with a similar affirmation:

ΠΙΣΤΕΥΟΜΕΝ ΕΙΣ ΕΝΑ ΘΕΟΝ
ΠΑΤΕΡΑ ΠΑΝΤΟΚΡΑΤΟΡΑ
ΠΟΙΗΤΗΝ ΟΥΡΑΝΟΥ ΚΑΙ ΓΗΣ
ΟΡΑΤΩΝ ΤΕ ΠΑΝΤΩΝ ΚΑΙ ΑΟΡΑΤΩΝ

WE BELIEVE IN ONE GOD
FATHER ALL-POWERFUL
MAKER OF HEAVEN AND EARTH
OF ALL THINGS SEEN AND UNSEEN

—Nicene Creed[10]

The Nicene Creed claims, as Genesis 1:1 claimed, that the one God is the "maker of the heavens and the earth," but it expanded this claim by adding "of all things seen and unseen." There was a tendency in the Greek-speaking world to value the "unseen" world, the spiritual world, as the truest and best, with the "seen" or material world as a lesser and perhaps evil world.

But in claiming that the one God is "the maker of the heavens and the earth, of all things seen and unseen," Christian communities asserted that **God is the creator of the material world as well as the spiritual world. The material world is God's good creation.** "And God saw that it was good" (Genesis 1:10, 12, 18, 21, 25). "God saw everything that he had made, and indeed, it was very good" (Genesis 1:31; see also Psalm 19:1 and Romans 1:20). This affirmation of the goodness of the material creation is a cardinal claim that Christian communities have made.[11] Without it, Christian belief in the material reality of Jesus' human body would make little sense.[12]

---

10. The text of the Nicene Creed is given as in Pelikan and Hotchkiss, *Creeds and Confessions*, 1:162.

11. The assertion in the Nicene Creed that God is the creator of the material world resulted from a long tension between proto-orthodox Christian communities, on the one hand, and other communities that did not value the material world and often ascribed its existence to an evil god or demiurge; see Ehrman, *Lost Christianities*, 122–24.

12. In comparison to this section of *A Deeper Christian Faith*, see the section "The Pyramid of Creation" in Joint Commission of Churches in Turkey, *Christianity* (34–35).

The Fear of יהוה

Look into an ancient world, this time into an old book called *Mishle Shlomoh* or Proverbs:

תחלת חכמה יראת יהוה

THE FEAR OF יהוה
IS THE BEGINNING OF WISDOM

—Proverbs 9:10

We respond to God with fear and worship. It might be nice to say that "fear" in this case does not mean anything as funky as "horror" or "dread" or "weirdness." It might be nice, but the truth is that the Hebrew word translated "fear" really does carry those meanings. The beginning of wisdom is to recognize the weirdness, the otherness, the strangeness, the holiness of God. The word can also mean that God is "awesome," but not in the cheery sense that "awesome" carries these days. It means that God is "awe-inspiring," something that causes us to tremble in fear.

God is weird, and men and women claim to have sensed the weird reality of God.[13] I don't just mean back in ye olden Bible times. When I was in Oxford, I heard a cell biologist casually say, after professing his atheism, that when he observed a cell and thought of the myriad structures and actions it took for a single cell to function, "I get this funny feeling." The most basic form of religious experience is the "funny feeling" that there's something greater than ourselves out there.[14]

Poetry and other literature can express this sense of wonder, sometimes better than prosaic descriptions of it. This excerpt from Kenneth Grahame's classic children's tale *The Wind in the Willows* envisions a dialogue between two characters after encountering a divine being. Grahame's two humanized characters Rat and Mole express the kind of religious awe that is like fear and yet at the same time utterly fascinating and lovely:

"Rat!" he found breath to whisper, shaking. "Are you afraid?"

---

13. World Council of Churches Faith and Order Commission, *Confessing the One Faith*, the commentary following ¶ 27.

14. A concept explored phenomenologically in the early twentieth century by William James in *Varieties of Religious Experience* and by Rudolph Otto in *The Idea of the Holy*.

"Afraid?" murmured the Rat, his eyes shining with unutterable love. "Afraid! Of *Him*? O, never, never! And yet—and yet—O, Mole, I am afraid!"

Then the two animals, crouching to the earth, bowed their heads and did worship.[15]

Early twentieth-century social scientists and philosophers such as William James and Rudolf Otto spoke of common religious experiences. A research project that began at Manchester College, Oxford, in the 1960s and has continued to the present time has shown that people regularly claim to have experiences that they identify as religious experiences. It has also shown something that might be uncomfortable for churchy people: it has shown that **people have these religious experiences regardless of whether they go to church, regardless of denominational affiliations or traditional religious affiliations, and across the supposed divide between "religious" and "secular" people.**[16]

But I have come to know this not just from social-scientific studies. When I served on the faculty of Wesley Theological Seminary in Washington DC, I got to know artists in a working art studio that is part of the Henry Luce III Center for Arts and Religion in the theological campus there. Many of the artists I met were not traditionally religious people, but they described vivid experiences of transcendence, experiences they struggled to express in their art. Some of them confided to me that they could not find in traditional churches anything like the depth of religious experience they found in their art.[17]

---

15. See the chapter entitled "The Piper at the Gates of Dawn" in Grahame, *Annotated Wind in the Willows*, 177.

16. The Religious Experience Research Unit was founded at Oxford University by Alister Hardy in 1969. Renamed as the Religious Experience Research Centre, the project continued at Westminster College, Oxford (now Westminster Institute of Oxford Brookes University) between 1989 and 1999, when it was transferred to the University of Wales, Lampeter, and has continued there as The Alister Hardy Religious Experience Research Centre. Some of the research developed by this Centre has been summarized by Wesley J. Wildman in *Religious and Spiritual Experiences*. Wildman himself concludes that religious and spiritual experiences do not confirm the existence of God, but rather "testify to the beauty and complexity of the world we treasure and strive to enrich" (264). The book summarizes a number of studies indicating the regularity of such experiences.

17. The Henry Luce III Center for Arts and Religion at Wesley Theological Seminary was founded by Catherine Kapikian, who insisted that the Center should not only have an art gallery but should also have a working studio for artists. See their website at http://luceartsandreligion.org.

When people—not just artists—cross the accustomed limits of their experience as human beings, they are most likely to experience this sense of something greater than themselves. The death of a close friend or family member, for example, pushes us beyond the limits of our ordinary experience and beyond our ordinary abilities to cope. Such an experience can bring us to the realization that we have to rely on something greater than we ourselves possess. Recognizing our own destructive tendencies, such as dependencies on alcohol or other drugs, can force us to admit that we cannot heal ourselves, that we need what folks in twelve-step movements call a "higher power." But simply stepping outside of our ordinary routines, for example, to contemplate the grandeur of the universe or to fast moderately, can also provoke such an experience.

Cosmopolitan God

The experience of something greater than ourselves leads to the sense that **God is not just for our own tribe or nation**. Christianity inherited the religious passion of Judaism for the oneness of God, and it also inherited a growing sense among people who thought of themselves as "cosmopolitans" (world citizens) that there is one God over all the nations of the earth. They had begun to think of traditional gods not necessarily as false deities, but as the way simpler people thought about various aspects of God.[18]

The New Testament describes these folks with a word that means "devout" or "reverent," those who "fear God." It is often translated "God-fearers," and these gentile "God-fearers" were often attracted to Christian belief (Acts 10:2, 22, 35; 13:16, 26).[19] They had already begun to cultivate "the fear of יהוה" that is "the beginning of wisdom."

Worship

The ancient Christian book called the Acts of the Apostles says that some of these gentile God-fearers worshiped with Jews in their synagogues (Acts 13:15–16). **We cultivate the fear of God, reverence toward God, not only as individuals but also as communities**. We worship.

18. Peters, *Harvest of Hellenism*, 133–40, 461–70.

19. Kittel and Friedrich, *Theological Dictionary of the New Testament*, 9:212–13, s.v. "Φοβέω."

Consider another text that appears in the book called *Devarim*, or Deuteronomy, and also in the book called *Shemot*, or Exodus:

אנכי יהוה אלהיך אשר הוצאתיך
מארץ מצרים מבית עבדים
לא יהיה־לך אלהים אחרים על־פני

I AM יהוה YOUR GOD
WHO BROUGHT YOU OUT OF THE LAND OF EGYPT
OUT OF THE HOUSE OF SLAVERY
YOU SHALL HAVE NO OTHER GODS
BEFORE ME

Exodus 20:2–3

Worship expresses what we value above all else. "You shall have no other gods before me." The word "you" in this command was plural, it was addressed to a community. The community was solemnly told that they could put nothing before God. They owed their final allegiance or worship to God alone.

The Protestant Reformer Martin Luther commented on this passage, "That to which your heart clings and entrusts itself is, I say, really your God."[20] No atheists are allowed by this claim: **everyone has something "to which [their] heart clings and entrusts itself."** We could paraphrase that to say that everyone has something that they value above everything else, everyone has something they worship, whether they call it "God" or not.

The Mystery of God and the Problem with Words

These words appear in the book of the prophet Isaiah:

קדוש קדוש קדוש יהוה צבאות
מלא כל־הארץ כבודו

HOLY HOLY HOLY
IS יהוה OF HOSTS

20. Luther's comment on the First Commandment is from the Larger Catechism, given in Tappert, *Book of Concord*, 365.

THE WHOLE EARTH IS FULL
OF HIS GLORY

Isaiah 6:3

This passage describes an ecstatic experience, an experience in which a person feels as if they're "standing outside of" themselves and gifted with new insight. The prophet claimed that he saw יהוה in the temple. Weird beings called *seraphim* with six wings flew around chanting that יהוה is holy, and they sang that the glory of יהוה filled the whole earth. The whole place shook and was filled with smoke. The prophet responded with appropriate fear: "Woe is me!"

Passages like this one from the book of the prophet Isaiah suggest that **there is an irreducible mystery at the heart of our faith in God that defies straightforward or literal description**. Our words fail, and in the end, we cannot really describe who God is. It would be, perhaps, like an artificial intelligence trying to describe a human being. The AI might get a lot of the details right, but in the end, humans would probably conclude that the AI really just didn't get it. As we try to describe God, God probably concludes that we don't get it, even though God is trying very hard to get through to us, even by becoming one of us.

Many of the words we use to describe God tell us, it turns out, more about who God is not than who God is. So, for example, everything we know is limited or finite, so we say that God is "infinite." That may sound like we know something about God, but in the end it simply means that God is not like the limited things we know. It tells us what we *don't* know about God, not much about what we know. Everything we know is limited in time, so we say that God is "eternal"; but that simply means that God is not like the temporal things we know.

We know just a little of what power means, so we say that God is "omnipotent" or "all-powerful," as in the words of the Nicene Creed quoted above. But in the end, that just says that God's power is not like the limited power that we know. In truth, we know just a little, so we say that God is "omniscient," "all-knowing" as if we know what that means. But we can't: we just know that God's knowledge is not limited like the knowledge that we have.

This is not merely a philosophy lesson. It's one of the ancient spiritual practices by which Christians have meditated on God's glory. It is traditionally called the *via negationis*, the "way of negation" or the "way of denial," and it means that **we meditate on God by negating words and ideas that describe things familiar to us, and then by considering how God transcends each of these things.**[21]

Here's a challenging example of the problem with words: does God "exist" like other things? Some very pious Christians have wondered if one of the things true of us and perhaps not true of God in quite the same way is "existence." We exist, and so do trees, and so does cancer. But does God "exist" in the same way that we "exist" and in precisely the same way that trees and cancer "exist"?

The prince of medieval theologians, the devout **Saint Thomas Aquinas**, did not hesitate to say that God does not "exist" in quite the same way in which you and I and trees and cancer exist. God exists, Thomas believed, in an exalted way that we cannot come close to comprehending. We can only understand the existence of God by an analogy, like a mathematical proportion, to things that we know more directly.[22]

I don't mean to suggest that it's common in Christian communities to doubt whether God exists. Far from it. I do mean to suggest that there's a sense in which our atheist and agnostic friends might be profoundly right and even profoundly pious when they say that God does not "exist." If they mean that God does not exist precisely as you and I and trees and cancer exist—and isn't that what most people mean when they say "exist"?—then perhaps we should commend their pious meditations on the mystery of God.[23] And moreover, many understandings of God doubted by agnostics and disbelieved by atheists have been doubted and disbelieved by faithful Jews, Christians, and Muslims for centuries.

21. Sophisticated expressions of this meditative technique were developed in the medieval School of St. Victor: see Knowles, *Evolution of Medieval Thought*, 141–47.

22. Thomas Aquinas raised the issue of "proportionality" or "analogy" in speaking of God in the *Summa Theologiae* 1.13.5, where he discussed the "names" of God (nouns [*nomina*] applied to God). Words applied to God cannot be "univocal" with words that describe other things—that is, they cannot mean precisely the same thing as words applied to created things. On the other hand, words applied to God are not "equivocal," meaning nothing at all the same as words applied to other things. He maintained, then, that words applied to God are used in a proportional or analogous way: not metaphorically, but in a real proportion to what we actually know. See Aquinas, *Summa Theologiae*, 1:67–68.

23. In comparison to this section of *A Deeper Christian Faith*, see the section "The Mind Cannot Comprehend God" of Joint Commission of Churches in Turkey, *Christianity*, 23–24.

I would say—and please note the first-person singular in this case—that we worship God not because God's existence has been demonstrated or proven. We worship God, we trust in God, we believe in God, because we dare to allow that **there is**—there "exists," if you will—**an irreducible mystery to the universe, and our lives are wrapped up in it**. It's weird. We can't escape it. **We worship**.

The Nature of God as Self-Giving Love

Given all the problems with language describing God, how close can we as human beings come towards understanding the deep, eternal nature of God? The first letter of St. John makes this remarkable claim:

Ο ΜΗ ΑΓΑΠΩΝ

ΟΥΚ ΕΓΝΩ ΤΟΝ ΘΕΟΝ

ΟΤΙ Ο ΘΕΟC ΑΓΑΠΗ ΕCΤΙΝ

WHOEVER DOES NOT LOVE

DOES NOT KNOW GOD

FOR GOD IS LOVE

1 John 4:8

As pleasant as it sounds, this is not greeting-card wisdom: the verb and noun translated "love" in this verse is *agapē*, a word the New Testament Scriptures use to describe the self-giving love of God shown in Christ's self-giving offering for us. The New Testament Scriptures refer to "the Son of God, who loved me and gave himself for me" (Gal 2:20), and they urge Christians to "live in love, as Christ loved us and gave himself up for us, a fragrant offering and sacrifice to God" (Eph 5:2). **As Christians understand it, the Scriptures reveal the unchanging nature of God as self-giving love**.

Both the Jewish as well as Christian Scriptures reveal the unchanging nature of God as self-giving love. They reveal that a kind of "suffering" is part of God's self-giving. I know a rabbi who has taught for decades at Garrett-Evangelical Theological Seminary on the campus of Northwestern University. Rabbi Schaalman was speaking one year on *Yom Ha-Shoah*, the day of remembrance of the *Shoah*, the Holocaust of Jews in the Second World War. He said that he had become convinced that God "suffers" in the sense that God somehow participates in the suffering of God's people. The rabbi worried that perhaps his view of God had been influenced by the Christians with whom he had worked at the seminary. But, on reflection, he came to believe that this was not only a Christian view of God, **it was a thoroughly biblical view of God, to believe that God is eternally self-giving and eternally suffering on behalf of God's people.**[24]

The self-giving love of God is the central thread of this book: the love that God has shown to us, and the love that we return to God. The next chapter will consider the basic Christian message, the "good news" or gospel, as the preeminent expression of God's self-giving love for human beings.

---

24. I am grateful to Rabbi Herman Schaalman for checking the text here, and his permission for me to refer to it.

CHAPTER 2

Holy Gospel

I want to invite you to a deeper Christian faith. **At the heart of this faith is a sacred message that reveals the eternal self-giving love that is the nature of God. Christians call this message the "gospel" or "good news" about Jesus Christ.**[1] As we shall see, the gospel would shape the collection of books that Christians call the New Testament, and it has been the consistent focus of Christian celebration through the centuries.

Transmitting the Gospel

How did we receive the gospel? It is not only in the words of the New Testament. Before the gospel was written down, it was transmitted orally in early Christian communities. In the following passage from the first letter of the apostle Paul to the Corinthians, Paul described how the gospel message had been transmitted:

ΓΝωΡΙΖω ΔΕ ΥΜΙΝ ΑΔΕΛΦΟΙ
ΤΟ ΕΥΑΓΓΕΛΙΟΝ Ο ΕΥΗΓΓΕΛΙCΑΜΗΝ ΥΜΙΝ
Ο ΚΑΙ ΠΑΡΕΛΑΒΕΤΕ ΕΝ ω ΚΑΙ ΕCΤΗΚΑΤΕ

I REMIND YOU BROTHERS AND SISTERS
OF THE GOSPEL THAT I PREACHED TO YOU

---

1. Much of the material in this chapter is derived from my book on *The Gospel in Christian Traditions*. See also World Council of Churches Faith and Order Commission, *Confessing the One Faith*, ¶¶ 127–92.

WHICH YOU ALSO RECEIVED
IN WHICH YOU ALSO STAND

1 Corinthians 15:1

Before the Gospels of Matthew, Mark, Luke, and John were written, long before there was a New Testament, there was the gospel, this simple message about Jesus Christ. On the day of Pentecost, the day that witnessed the birth of the Christian community, Saint Peter proclaimed the message about Jesus Christ (Acts 2:14–36). The Christian faith existed before the New Testament was written, so as strange as this may sound, while it is possible to have the Christian faith without the New Testament, according to the New Testament itself, it is impossible to have the Christian faith without the gospel. The gospel is the heart of the Christian faith.

This text from 1 Corinthians was eventually written down, but **it holds within it a number of signs of the transmission of oral texts**. It wasn't easy to remember texts accurately without writing them down. In the ancient world, a particularly important text would be solemnly recited out loud in the presence of witnesses. The recitation might begin with a declaration that the words to be recited were just such an important text. This passage in 1 Corinthians contains two such declarations: "I remind you, brothers and sisters, of the good news that I preached to you, which you also received" (verse 1), and then "For I handed on to you as of first importance that which I also received" (verse 3). In these cases, the word "you" is plural, indicating that this was an act of transmission to a community of people. The words translated "to hand on" and "to receive" were technical terms in the Greek language to indicate the transmission of oral texts by "handing on" (reciting the message) and "receiving" (hearing the message).[2]

In some cases, the transmission of an oral text was accompanied by blessings pronounced on those who recited the text correctly and curses pronounced on those who distorted the text. Although Paul did not issue blessings or curses with this recitation of the gospel message in 1 Corinthians 15, he did elsewhere. In the letter to the Galatians, Paul pronounced a solemn double curse on anyone who would distort the gospel message:

---

2. In Kittel and Friedrich, *Theological Dictionary of the New Testament*, 2:171 (παραδίδωμι, s.v. δίδωμι); and 4:13–14 (παραλαμβάνω, s.v. λαμβάνω).

> I am astonished that you are so quickly deserting the one who called you in the grace of Christ and are turning to a different gospel—not that there is another gospel, but there are some who are confusing you and want to pervert the gospel of Christ. But even if we or an angel from heaven should proclaim to you a gospel contrary to what we proclaimed to you, let that one be accursed! As we have said before, so now I repeat, if anyone proclaims to you a gospel contrary to what you received, let that one be accursed! (Galatians 1:6–9)

Although he did not issue blessings or curses in the passage from 1 Corinthians, Paul appealed to witnesses, another means of vouching for the authenticity of an oral text. The particular issue Paul addressed in this section of his letter to the Corinthians was the matter of Christian belief about the resurrection of the dead. After listing witnesses to Jesus' resurrection, he added a concluding formula of tradition: "Whether I or others [who proclaimed the gospel], thus we have proclaimed, and thus you [plural] have believed" (1 Cor 15:11).

This passage from 1 Corinthians and a parallel passage about the Lord's Supper in chapter 11 of that book (see chapter 4) may be the oldest written words about Jesus. They were written down around the decade of the 50s AD, within twenty-five years of the events of Jesus' death and resurrection that they describe.[3] As Paul himself noted, witnesses to these events were still alive when he wrote these words. Most importantly, Paul appealed to these words as words that he himself and the Corinthian congregation had already heard or "received."

This pattern of the oral handing-on of the gospel message continued in Christian communities after the New Testament was written down. **New converts were told the gospel message in a set form of words they were asked to memorize and then told to recite as their own profession of faith.** Saint Augustine of Hippo, writing around AD 400, described the conversion of the Neoplatonic philosopher Marius Victorinus and then Victorinus's profession of Christian faith:

> Eventually the time came for making his profession of faith. At Rome those who are about to enter into your grace usually make their profession in a set form of words which they learn by heart and recite from a raised platform in view of the faithful.[4]

3. Theissen and Merz, *Historical Jesus*, 488; see the broader discussion of this passage, 486–90.

4. Augustine, *Confessions*, 8:160; see the Latin text given in Augustine, *Les Confessions*, 14:18.

This way of hearing and reciting the good news was the basis of early Christian creeds, as we will see below. And we shall see in the next chapter that it continues as one of the ways by which Christians are formed in the faith and by which they profess their faith.

The Content of the Gospel

What, then, was the content of the gospel or "good news" that Paul recited? He gave the content he had received in the following words from his first letter to the Corinthians:

ΟΤΙ ΧΡΙΣΤΟΣ ΑΠΕΘΑΝΕΝ
ΥΠΕΡ ΤΩΝ ΑΜΑΡΤΙΩΝ ΗΜΩΝ
ΚΑΤΑ ΤΑΣ ΓΡΑΦΑΣ
ΚΑΙ ΟΤΙ ΕΤΑΦΗ
ΚΑΙ ΟΤΙ ΕΓΗΓΕΡΤΑΙ ΤΗ ΗΜΕΡΑ ΤΗ ΤΡΙΤΗ
ΚΑΤΑ ΤΑΣ ΓΡΑΦΑΣ

THAT CHRIST DIED FOR OUR SINS
ACCORDING TO THE SCRIPTURES
AND THAT HE WAS BURIED
AND THAT HE WAS RAISED ON THE THIRD DAY
ACCORDING TO THE SCRIPTURES

1 Corinthians 15:3–4

The message was very simple indeed. **The gospel announced Christ's death, Christ's burial, and Christ's resurrection**. The point about Christ's burial was a way of emphasizing the reality of Christ's death, so that the death and resurrection of Jesus were the two cardinal points of the gospel message.

The gospel that Paul received and transmitted stated that **both the death and resurrection of Christ were "according to the scriptures."** This could not have referred to what we call the New Testament Scriptures. When Paul wrote down these words, probably in the decade of the 50s AD, there simply was no New Testament. The expression "the Scriptures" referred to the Hebrew and Aramaic writings that Jews call the *Tanach* and that Christians would call the Old Testament.

It was enormously important that Paul claimed that the gospel was "according to the scriptures." I don't think he meant to say that specific Old Testament passages were fulfilled by Jesus' death and resurrection, or at least not that alone. He meant that the revelation of the one God in the Christian gospel was consistent with the revelation of the one God in the Jewish Scriptures.

Why was it important to say this? Many ancient religious communities maintained that the God of Jesus was entirely different from the deity described in the Jewish Scriptures.[5] And if Jesus' God was not the God of the Jews, they could believe that the material creation was *not* the work of "the Father of our Lord Jesus Christ" (2 Cor 1:3; 11:31; Eph 1:3; 1 Pet 1:3). Christian groups who maintained the gospel message Paul received and transmitted (groups that in retrospect we call orthodox or "proto-orthodox" Christian communities) affirmed that the gospel is "according to the scriptures." That is, **they affirmed the strong connection to the Jewish Scriptures and the belief expressed in the Jewish Scriptures that the material creation is the good work of the one God**. These early Christian communities maintained that, in fact, the one God had entered into the reality of the material world in the person of Jesus Christ of Nazareth.

Although the early form of the gospel message Paul transmitted did not make explicit the direct identification of Jesus Christ as the one God, **it did associate Christ's work with the divine work of forgiveness**: "Christ died *for our sins* according to the scriptures." Christ's work was instrumental in God's work of saving or healing humankind.

In his letter to the Philippians, Paul gave a snippet of what may be an ancient Christian hymn, which says that Christ,

> THOUGH HE WAS IN THE FORM OF GOD
> DID NOT REGARD EQUALITY WITH GOD
> AS SOMETHING TO BE EXPLOITED
> BUT EMPTIED HIMSELF TAKING THE FORM OF A SLAVE
> AND BEING BORN IN HUMAN LIKENESS
> AND BEING FOUND IN HUMAN FORM
> HE HUMBLED HIMSELF

---

5. This describes the views of Marcionites and some other second-century groups.

AND BECAME OBEDIENT TO THE POINT OF DEATH
EVEN DEATH ON A CROSS

Philippians 2:6–8

The gospel about Jesus Christ is a message about the mysterious self-emptying love of God.[6] This passage also shows that the work of God in Christ reveals who God is and has been forever: eternal, self-giving love.

The Gospel and the Christian Bible

The gospel message shaped the Christian Bible in the earliest Christian centuries. Proto-orthodox Christian communities read the Old Testament as Scripture, since they believed that the key elements of the gospel, Christ's death and resurrection, were both "according to the [Old Testament] Scriptures." Jewish communities had arranged the Old Testament books with the Torah first (Genesis, Exodus, Leviticus, Numbers, and Deuteronomy), followed by the writings of the prophets, then followed by other writings, including the Psalms and Proverbs. Christian communities kept the Torah first, but placed the prophets last, so that the prophetic message connected the Old Testament writings to the New Testament that followed immediately after them. In ordering the books in this way, Christian communities structured the Bible so that the Old Testament could be seen as directly foreshadowing the gospel message.

At the time of the reformations in the 1500s, most Protestant churches decided to use only those Old Testament books and portions of other books that existed in Hebrew manuscripts. In preferring these writings, Protestants rejected a body of literature that existed only in Greek manuscripts and are still utilized by Catholic and Orthodox churches. The disputed writings are called the **Apocrypha** or the Deuterocanonical writings.

The gospel transmitted by Saint Paul and by proto-orthodox Christian communities also **shaped the list or canon of books of the New Testament**.[7] Christian communities in the 100s AD utilized many books that were not eventually recognized as Scripture by Christian churches.[8] The

---

6. Kittel and Friedrich, *Theological Dictionary of the New Testament*, 3:661 (κενόω, s.v. "κενός").

7. Pelikan, *Christian Tradition*, 5:112–16.

8. This is the general subject of Ehrman, *Lost Christianities*; see the first 6 chapters,

books that were chosen to be read in these early Christian communities affirmed the connection between the Old and New Testament, and affirmed the reality of Christ's suffering, death, and resurrection.[9] Proto-orthodox communities also favored books connected directly to the Palestinian and Pauline communities in which Christianity originated.

But bound volumes containing New Testament books were a later development. The earliest Christian communities typically had access to only a few of the writings that churches later acknowledged to be Scripture. Some early Christian writings reveal that their authors only had access to a few New Testament works, and sometimes only a few Old Testament books as well.[10]

By the middle of the 100s AD, a consensus was developing in proto-orthodox Christian churches about a core of Christian Scriptures. This consensus included the four Gospels we now have in Christian Bibles, the Acts of the Apostles, and seven or so letters of Saint Paul.[11] The value of other writings was debated for a century or more. It was not until AD 367 that Saint Athanasius of Alexandria gave the precise list of twenty-seven writings that Christian communities today include in the New Testament.[12] Even then, **the gospel message continued to serve as the key to understanding the meaning of the Christian Scriptures, the basic message that gave unity to the whole of the Christian Bible.**[13]

The Gospel in the Creeds

Christian communities continued to solemnly recite this simple message about Jesus, the gospel, as the core of their beliefs. The message was taught to candidates for baptism, and it came to be recited by congregations in worship. The following Latin words reflect an early Christian baptismal creed used in Western churches that came to be called **the Apostles' Creed:**

13–134.

9. Pelikan, *Christian Tradition*, 1:110–12.

10. For example, William R. Schoedel shows that the letters of Ignatius of Antioch reveal direct knowledge of some of the letters of Paul and the Gospel according to Matthew, but little else in the New Testament canon: Schoedel, *Ignatius of Antioch*, 9–10.

11. Muratorian fragment, in *Enchiridion Biblicum*, nos. 1–7; see the English translation in Bettenson, *Documents of the Christian Church*, 28–29.

12. See Athanasius's Festal Letter 39 in *Enchiridion Biblicum*, nos. 14–15.

13. Pelikan, *Credo*, 142–57; Young, *Virtuoso Theology*, 60–61.

Holy Gospel

pΛSSUS SUB PONTIO PILΛTO
CRUCIFIXUS MORTUUS ET SEPULTUS
DESCENDIT ΛD INFEROS
TERTIΛ DIE RESURREXIT Λ MORTUIS

HE SUFFERED UNDER PONTIUS PILΛTE
WΛS CRUCIFIED DEΛD ΛND BURIED
HE DESCENDED TO THE UNDERWORLD
ON THE THIRD DΛY HE ROSE FROM THE DEΛD

The Apostles' Creed[14]

The gospel message was the nucleus around which Christian creeds developed. The Apostles' Creed affirmed that Christ "suffered under Pontius Pilate." The expression "under Pontius Pilate" was a Roman means of locating an event in a specific time and in a particular geographic area.

The Apostles' Creed, consistent with earlier expressions of the gospel message, affirms Christ's crucifixion, death, and burial. It then states that **Christ "descended to the underworld."** The word for "underworld" was a common expression. It did not imply the place of judgment or damnation suggested by the traditional English translation, "he descended into hell." To say that Christ "descended to the underworld" was another way of affirming that Christ truly died, just as the statement that Christ "was buried" in 1 Corinthians 15:4 also claimed the material reality of Christ's death.[15]

Some later Western Christians objected to the words "descended into hell," because in English and perhaps other languages it implied that Christ went to the place reserved for condemned sinners. The Methodist churches in which I was raised omitted the phrase from the Creed for this reason, although it is now being restored as people understand that it denotes the reality of Christ's human death.

---

14. The text of the Apostles' Creed is given as in Pelikan and Hotchkiss, *Creeds and Confessions*, 1:669, using the alternate reading *inferos* in place of *inferna*.

15. A related doctrine is the teaching that Christ went into the place of the dead to free those who were held captive there until his coming, the teaching referred to in historic English texts as the "harrowing of hell." But I am regarding that as a further extension of the teaching expressed here, that Christ truly died as a human being and in this sense went to the place of the dead.

The Nicene Creed (fourth century AD), common to Eastern and Western Christian communities, makes very similar claims about the basic gospel narrative:

ⲤⲦⲀⲨⲢⲰⲐⲈⲚⲦⲀ ⲦⲈ ⲨⲠⲈⲢ ⲎⲘⲰⲚ
ⲈⲠⲒ ⲠⲞⲚⲦⲒⲞⲨ ⲠⲒⲖⲀⲦⲞⲨ
ⲔⲀⲒ ⲠⲀⲐⲞⲚⲦⲀ ⲔⲀⲒ ⲦⲀⲫⲈⲚⲦⲀ
ⲔⲀⲒ ⲀⲚⲀⲤⲦⲀⲚⲦⲀ ⲦⲎ ⲦⲢⲒⲦⲎ ⲎⲘⲈⲢⲀ
ⲔⲀⲦⲀ ⲦⲀⲤ ⲄⲢⲀⲫⲀⲤ

HE WAS CRUCIFIED FOR US
UNDER PONTIUS PILATE
AND SUFFERED AND WAS BURIED
AND ROSE ON THE THIRD DAY
ACCORDING TO THE SCRIPTURES

Nicene Creed[16]

To say that Christ was "crucified for us" recalls the words of the primitive gospel in 1 Corinthians 15:3, that Christ "died for our sins in accordance with the scriptures." To say that Christ "rose on the third day according to the scriptures" replicated exactly the words of the primitive gospel in 1 Corinthians 15:4. But these words in the Nicene Creed were not necessarily copied from 1 Corinthians: the primitive gospel message had continued to be repeated orally and solemnly in Christian assemblies, and by the time the Nicene Creed was composed, these words were part of the fabric of Christian life.[17]

The Gospel Acclaimed

In addition to the expression of the gospel in the creeds, forms of Christian worship have also incorporated brief ways of expressing this most basic Christian message. The liturgies of Eastern Orthodox churches include a congregational acclamation of the work of Christ as part of their service for the Lord's Supper (see chapter 4 on the "Holy Feast"). The Coptic

16. The text of the Nicene Creed is given as in Pelikan and Hotchkiss, *Creeds and Confessions*, 1:162.

17. On the importance of continuing oral traditions, see Joint Commission of Churches in Turkey, *Christianity*, 15–16.

Orthodox Church, part of the family of Oriental Orthodox churches, uses the following acclamations that are said or chanted by the congregation. The fact that these acclamations are given in Greek and embedded in the Coptic-language liturgy suggests that they date from a very early period in the development of Egyptian Christianity, perhaps the fourth or fifth century, when Greek was still utilized:

ⲀⲘⲎⲚ ⲀⲘⲎⲚ ⲀⲘⲎⲚ
ⲦⲞⲚ ⲐⲀⲚⲀⲦⲞⲚ ⲤⲞⲨ ⲔⲨⲢⲒⲈ ⲔⲀⲦⲀⲄⲄⲈⲖⲞⲘⲈⲚ
ⲔⲀⲒ ⲦⲎⲚ ⲀⲄⲒⲀⲚ ⲤⲞⲨ ⲀⲚⲀⲤⲦⲀⲤⲒⲚ
ⲔⲀⲒ ⲦⲎⲚ ⲀⲚⲀⲖⲎⲮⲒⲚ ⲤⲞⲨ
ⲈⲚ ⲦⲞⲒⲤ ⲞⲨⲢⲀⲚⲞⲒⲤ ⲤⲞⲨ ⲞⲘⲞⲖⲞⲄⲞⲨⲘⲈⲚ
ⲤⲈ ⲨⲘⲚⲞⲨⲘⲈⲚ ⲤⲈ ⲈⲨⲖⲞⲄⲞⲨⲘⲈⲚ
ⲤⲞⲒ ⲈⲨⲬⲀⲢⲒⲤⲦⲞⲨⲘⲈⲚ ⲔⲨⲢⲒⲈ
ⲔⲀⲒ ⲆⲈⲞⲘⲈⲐⲀ ⲤⲞⲨ Ⲟ ⲐⲈⲞⲤ ⲎⲘⲰⲚ

AMEN AMEN AMEN
YOUR DEATH O LORD WE PROCLAIM
AND YOUR HOLY RESURRECTION
AND YOUR ASCENSION IN YOUR HEAVEN WE CONFESS
WE PRAISE YOU
WE BLESS YOU
WE THANK YOU O LORD
AND WE BESEECH YOU O OUR GOD

Memorial Acclamations in the Coptic Liturgy[18]

Since the 1970s, the Catholic Church and many Protestant have churches incorporated acclamations such as these in their celebration of the Lord's Supper. In the Catholic Mass, the priest says, "The mystery of faith," and the congregation replies:

WHEN WE EAT THIS BREAD
AND DRINK THIS CUP
WE PROCLAIM YOUR DEATH

18. See the rather old-fashioned English translation in Ishak, *Complete Translation*, 95. I have regularized the Greek given in Coptic script in this passage.

LORD JESUS
UNTIL YOU COME IN GLORY

Memorial Acclamations in the Mass[19]

In 1970, a version of this was adopted in an English translation of the Mass, and it has come to be utilized by Anglican and Protestant communities as a way of summarizing "the mystery of faith":

CHRIST HAS DIED
CHRIST IS RISEN
CHRIST WILL COME AGAIN

Memorial Acclamations in the Great Prayer of Thanksgiving[20]

Jesus Christ as God

A Roman official named Pliny happened to be a friend of the Emperor Trajan. Among other chitchat he reported to the emperor from Asia Minor in the 110s AD, along with his account of stabbing a hapless rabbit with his stylus, he commented on a new religious group that had come to his attention. He wrote in a letter to Trajan that **it was the custom of the Christians he observed "to sing a song to Christ as to a god."**[21] Pliny was one of the first non-Christian observers to spot a consistent trait of Christian communities: their worship of Jesus Christ as God.[22]

We've already seen that the gospel tradition in 1 Corinthians 15 was written down in the decade of the 50s AD and reflected oral traditions that Paul and the Corinthian congregation had "received" earlier than that. Consider another letter written in the name of the apostle Paul to a Christian community in the town of Colossae. The town itself was destroyed by

19. Catholic Church, *Sacramentary*, 506, 511, 514, 520.

20. These acclamations are cited as they appear in the Catholic liturgy (see the previous reference), in the Episcopal Church, *Book of Common Prayer*, 363; and in United the Methodist Church, *United Methodist Hymnal*, 10, 14, and 16. As of 2011, this form of acclamation was no longer utilized in Catholic churches in favor of the literal translation of the Latin text of the Mass given above.

21. Letter of Pliny the Younger to the Emperor Trajan, cited from Mynors, *C. Plini Caecili*, 339; the translation is my own. See Wilken, "Christians as the Romans," 1:111–13.

22. World Council of Churches Faith and Order Commission, *Confessing the One Faith*, ¶¶ 90–126.

an earthquake in AD 60, so the letter to the Colossians is probably from the 50s AD. Here's how this letter describes Christ:

OTI EN ΑΥΤΟ ΚΑΤΟΙΚΕΙ
ΠΑΝ ΤΟ ΠΛΗΡΟΜΑ ΤΗC ΘΕΟΤΗΤΟC
CΟΜΑΤΙΚΟC

FOR IN HIM DWELLS
ALL THE FULLNESS OF DIVINITY
BODILY

Colossians 2:9

In Christ, the letter claimed, "all the fullness of divinity dwells bodily." **The letter used even more extravagant language to describe Christ as a divine being:**

> He is the image of the invisible God, the first-born of all creation; for in him all things in heaven and on earth were created, things visible and invisible, whether thrones or dominions or rulers or powers—all things have been created through him and for him. He himself is before all things and in him all things hold together . . . For in him all the fullness of God was pleased to dwell, and through him God was pleased to reconcile to himself all things, whether on earth or in heaven, by making peace through the blood of his cross. (Colossians 1:15–17, 19–20)

The word "image" at the beginning of this passage is *eikon*, the word also translated "icon," so Jesus Christ marked the space-time coordinates in which the fullness of God dwelt. He was the visible "icon" of the invisible God.

The letters of Paul, the earliest written Christian documents, are imbued with devotion to Jesus Christ appropriate to a divine being. Paul wrote of the Christian communities "who in every place call on the name of our Lord Jesus Christ" (1 Cor 1:2). His letters often begin with a prayer for grace from God the Father and Jesus Christ: "Grace to you and peace from God our Father and the Lord Jesus Christ" (Gal 1:3). His letters typically conclude with ascriptions of glory: "to the only wise God, through Jesus Christ, to whom be the glory forever" (Rom 16:26). He reverenced Jesus

Christ as a divine being. It's not surprising that Pliny found the Christians of Asia Minor in the 110s AD singing "a song to Christ as to a god."[23]

Despite these indications of reverence for Jesus as a divine being, **some have objected to the Christian practice of worshiping Jesus Christ on the grounds that Jesus himself did not explicitly identify himself as God in the Gospels**. It is true that in the Gospels Jesus spoke of himself in a consistently cryptic or mysterious manner. When Peter finally confessed that Jesus was the "anointed one" or Christ, Jesus "sternly ordered them not to tell anyone about him" (Mark 8:30). So Jesus himself was not intent on making his own identity clear to everyone immediately, and the Gospels of Matthew, Mark, and Luke depict Jesus' followers as only slowly beginning to recognize who he actually was.

The Gospel according to Matthew concludes with an appearance of the resurrected Christ in the midst of his followers, and it says that "When they saw him, they worshiped him, but some doubted" (Matthew 28:17). The word "worshiped" here literally means that they bent their knees as a sign of respect or reverence. Even this term wouldn't absolutely have to mean that they recognized him as a divine being, and even then, as the Gospel matter-of-factly states, "some doubted."

It's kind of disappointing if you believe that this group of Jesus' followers were present at Jesus' baptism when the heavens opened and God said, "You are my Son, the Beloved; with you I am well pleased" (Mark 1:9–11). And had they not heard about Jesus' going up on the mountain of transfiguration, when his appearance was miraculously transformed and God said, "This is my Son, the Beloved. Listen to him" (9:2–8)? And the miracles and the forgiveness of sins, and a resurrection from the dead, and then, ho hum, "some doubted." What would it take to convince these people?

Apparently it took more than all that. Jesus did not come out and say, "OK, I am God." **He taught, as many ancient teachers did, by posing questions, suggesting analogies, and challenging students to figure out stuff on their own**. To take one example of Jesus' cryptic way of speaking about himself, Saint John the Baptist sent some of his disciples to ask Jesus, "Are you the one who is to come, or shall we wait for another?" (Matt 11:3). This question did not ask if Jesus was God; it asked if he was the Messiah. But Jesus' response to John, like his response to Peter, shows how he typically

---

23. On the New Testament's depiction of Jesus' divinity, see Hurtado, *Lord Jesus Christ*.

answered questions about his identity. He did not respond by saying, "Yes, OK, you got it right. I'm the one." He responded:

> Go and tell John what you hear and see: the blind receive their sight, the lame walk, the lepers are cleansed, the deaf hear, the dead are raised, and the poor have good news brought to them. (Matt 11:4–5)

And then he added, "And blessed is anyone who takes no offense at me" (11:6). Figure it out for yourselves. Meanwhile, a demon could say, "I know who you are, the Holy One of God" (Mark 1:24), and a Roman centurion exclaimed, "Truly this man was God's son" (Mark 15:39; Matt 27:54). They seem to have figured out for themselves who Jesus was without an explicit claim.

Jesus' cryptic way of speaking in the Gospels led some interpreters to think that the older material about Jesus depicted him as a wise human teacher, and only later material represented him as being God. In the time of Thomas Jefferson, for example, it was believed that one could snip out all the miraculous material from the Gospels, leaving Jesus as a really, really nice guy, and one could presume that this would represent the true Jesus, the earliest historical material about Jesus.

But this view, however popular, does not account for the chronology of the New Testament texts in which references to Jesus as divine appear in the earliest New Testament materials such as the letters of Paul. Heidelberg scholars Gerd Theissen and Annette Merz, introducing a massive overview of research on *The Historical Jesus* (1996), commented at the very beginning of their work that there are two basic sources for our knowledge about Jesus: the material from the Gospels and the material from Paul. They stated as a matter of fact that the material from Paul was written earlier than the material in the written Gospels. Then they pointed out that some interpreters doubt the veracity of the material from Paul because of "the pauline 'tendency' to see Jesus as a preexistent, mythical being."[24] You don't have to read far between the lines here to grasp the fact that **the oldest written material about Jesus is the material that represents him as "a preexistent, mythical being,"** not just a nice guy.

The worship of Jesus Christ is the most distinctive trait of historic Christian communities. It is the practice that most readily distinguishes Christian communities from Jewish and Muslim and other religious

24. Theissen and Merz, *Historical Jesus*, 17.

communities. The *Qur'ān*, for example, shares the Christian and Jewish worship of one God, and it even refers to Jesus as the Christ as well as a prophet, but it does not allow the worship of Jesus. One passage of the *Qur'ān*, has the following:

> And behold! Allah will say: "O Jesus the son of Mary! Did you say to men, 'worship me and my mother as gods in derogation of Allah'?" He will say: "Glory to You! Never could I say what I had no right (to say)." (*Qur'ān* sura 5)[25]

That is, God asks Jesus if Jesus had told humans to worship him and his mother. Jesus denies having said this, according to the *Qur'ān*.

The traditional Christian worship of Jesus Christ as God leads to an asymmetry between Christian worship, on the one hand, and Jewish and Muslim worship, on the other hand. Christians can generally participate in the prayers of Jewish and Muslim worship. But Muslims and Jews cannot straightforwardly participate in Christian worship when praise and prayers are offered to Jesus Christ. **The worship of Jesus Christ is the most distinctive mark of historic Christian communities**.

Father, Son, and Holy Spirit

The Christian faith emerged in an age when people were comfortable with the thought of multiple heavenly beings and multiple revelations of God even when they believed in one God. **The New Testament and other proto-orthodox writings consistently depict Christ and the Holy Spirit as heavenly beings to whom Christians offer worship and prayers**. Consider this blessing at the conclusion of Paul's second letter to the Corinthians:

Ⲏ ⲬⲀⲢⲓⲤ ⲦⲞⲨ ⲔⲨⲢⲒⲞⲨ ⲒⲎⲤⲞⲨ ⲬⲢⲒⲤⲦⲞⲨ
ⲔⲀⲒ Ⲏ ⲀⲄⲀⲠⲎ ⲦⲞⲨ ⲐⲈⲞⲨ
ⲔⲀⲒ Ⲏ ⲔⲞⲒⲚⲰⲚⲒⲀ ⲦⲞⲨ ⲀⲄⲒⲞⲨ ⲠⲚⲈⲨⲘⲀⲦⲞⲤ
ⲘⲈⲦⲀ ⲠⲀⲚⲦⲰⲚ ⲨⲘⲰⲚ

THE GRACE OF THE LORD JESUS CHRIST
AND THE LOVE OF GOD

---

25. *Qur'ān* sura 5 ("The Table Spread"), verse 116, in the translation of Ali, *Qur'ān*, 75. On Muslim beliefs about Jesus, see Ayoub, *Islam*, 37–39.

Holy Gospel

AND THE FELLOWSHIP OF THE HOLY SPIRIT
BE WITH ALL OF YOU

2 Corinthians 13:13

This is not the only passage where Christ and the Holy Spirit are invoked along with God, or God the Father. In chapter 8 of Paul's letter to the Romans, Paul spoke of Christ's prayer to *Abba*, "Father," and the way in which the Holy Spirit can make our prayer one with the prayer of the Son to the Father (Rom 8:15–17). At the conclusion of the Gospel according to Matthew, Jesus instructed his disciples to go into the world, "baptizing in the name of the Father and of the Son and of the Holy Spirit" (Matt 28:19). Moreover, Jesus prayed to the Father (for example, John 17:1, 5). The Father pronounced, "This is my Son, the Beloved" (Matt 3:17 and parallels). The Holy Spirit drove Jesus into the wilderness (Matt 4:1 and parallels). As early Christian creeds developed orally in the period after the New Testament, they were consistently organized around the threefold structure of belief in God the Father, belief in Jesus Christ, and belief in the Holy Spirit.[26]

Christian communities offered prayer to Christ and to the Holy Spirit at the same time as they affirmed that there is only one God. They don't seem to have worried too much about that—they just prayed and confessed their faith in one God, in Jesus Christ, and in the Holy Spirit. When forced to explain this further, Christian leaders developed language to describe the distinctness of Father, Son, and Holy Spirit as **three "persons" united in one God, one divine "stuff" or "substance,"** but no one presumed to know exactly what a divine "person" is or what the "stuff" or "substance" is that is God. "Person" was the term they agreed on to speak of the unique persons of the Father, the Son, and the Holy Spirit. "Stuff" or "substance" or "being" was the term (just one word in Greek) they used to describe the unity or oneness of God.[27] Deny that God is one in stuff or being and you've gone too far, resulting in tritheism, belief in three gods. Deny that the Holy Spirit, the Son, and the Father have personal relationships with each other, and you've gone too far, resulting in "modalism," the notion that the three persons are not really persons, but just different and perhaps temporary appearances or functions of the one God.

26. On ecumenical consensus in Trinitarian faith, see World Council of Churches Faith and Order Commission, *Confessing the One Faith*, ¶¶ 15–22.

27. The use of the word "stuff" as a less-technical-sounding translation for "substance" (οὐσία) was suggested by reading Stead, *Divine Substance*.

The essence of Christian teaching about the Trinity is not the use of the word "Trinity." Neither the New Testament nor the earliest Christian creeds use that word. It isn't about the words "stuff" or "substance" or "persons," even if the creeds do use those words. The essence of this teaching is **the practice of offering praise to the Father, the Son, and the Holy Spirit as one God**. Here's a way in which Christian communities offered this praise from time out of mind:

GLORIA PATRI
ET FILIO
ET SPIRITUI SANCTO
SICUT ERAT IN PRINCIPIO
ET NUNC ET SEMPER
ET IN SAECULA SAECULORUM
AMEN

GLORY TO THE FATHER
AND TO THE SON
AND TO THE HOLY SPIRIT
AS IT WAS IN THE BEGINNING
AND IS NOW AND ALWAYS
AND INTO THE AGES OF AGES
AMEN

An ancient Christian ascription, the *Gloria Patri*

Christ as Divine and Human

The earliest New Testament writings express reverence for Christ as a divine being. Christian communities had worshiped Jesus Christ from the earliest decades, and the Nicene Creed explicitly acknowledged Christ's identity as fully divine, "of the same substance as the Father." But at the same time, Christian communities never stopped believing that Jesus Christ was fully and completely human. He grew as a child; he wept at the death of a friend; he experienced hunger and thirst and temptation; he suffered and he died. We have seen above how the earliest Christian traditions embedded in the Scriptures made clear that his death was a genuine, material death: he "was buried," he "descended to the dead."

Christian leaders in the early centuries were intensely concerned to clarify how Christ could be simultaneously God and human, fully divine and fully a human being. Christian communities differed over how to express this mystery, and in fact some of the oldest divisions of the Christian churches date to the period of the 400s through the 600s AD, when churches struggled to define these issues. The issue they faced was not whether Christ was divine or human; the longstanding consensus of Christian communities affirmed both of these claims. The issue was how Christians could express both a) **the integrity of the divine and human in Christ**, and b) **the unity of divine and human in Christ**. Christian communities presupposed and continue to affirm today that Christ was fully human and fully divine, and that the divine and human in Christ were united in Christ's person.[28]

Ancient Christians approached these issues about the nature of Jesus Christ with an almost ferocious passion, perhaps akin to the passion with which many Christians today approach issues about homosexual practice or abortion. The passion with which Christians pursued these issues led to divisions between Christian communities, though we should be clear that accompanying these divisions were also cultural and geographical and linguistic differences between Christian communities and sometimes just rivalries between different groups of churches. The issues became very complicated, but we can summarize some of the main developments as follows.

- These issues came to focus on a particular way of honoring Saint Mary, Jesus' mother. Literally fulfilling the words of Mary recorded in Luke 1:48, "Surely, from now on all generations will call me blessed," Christian communities including historic Protestant churches have honored Mary by calling her **"the Blessed Virgin."**[29] Mary was, by all accounts, the mother of the human incarnation of Christ.

28. World Council of Churches Faith and Order Commission, *Confessing the One Faith*, ¶¶ 120–26. However, I do not see how this document could justify its claim that "All Christians share in the confession affirmed by the Council of Ephesus (431) that Mary is 'Theotokos,' the mother of him who is also God, through the creative work of the Spirit of God" (¶ 122). The Assyrian Church of the East has not affirmed the Blessed Virgin as *Theotokos*, nor have the confessions of many Protestant bodies (see the text following).

29. Augsburg Confession item 3 (in Pelikan and Hotchkiss, *Creeds and Confessions*, 2:60); Church of England, Articles of Religion 2 (in Pelikan and Hotchkiss, *Creeds and Confessions*, 2:528); Methodist Articles of Religion 2 (in Pelikan and Hotchkiss, *Creeds and Confessions*, 3:202).

- But **should Mary be called the "God-bearer" (Theotokos) or "the Mother of God"?** Those who emphasized the unity of divine and human in Jesus Christ answered affirmatively: Saint Mary was the mother of one person who was divine and human. She was "the Mother of God" in the sense that she was the mother of the one person who was divine and human.

- The great majority of Christian communities—including Eastern Orthodox churches, the Catholic Church, and eventually the historic Protestant churches—affirm language from the Council of Chalcedon (AD 451) that spoke of **two "natures" (divine and human natures) in the one "Person" of Jesus Christ.**[30] Consistent with this, Eastern Orthodox and Catholic churches and some historic Protestant communities also refer to Mary as "the God-bearer" or "Mother of God" in this sense.[31]

- Other Christian communities have not accepted the wording of the Council of Chalcedon. Those who emphasized the distinctness or integrity of divine and human in Christ could not accept that a human being could be "the Mother of God." The ancient **Assyrian Church of the East** believes that the formula of "one Person in two natures" does not sufficiently express the integrity and distinctness of divine and human in Christ. They honor Saint Mary, but do not refer to her as "God-bearer" or "Mother of God." The Assyrian Church of the East has been separate from other Christian communities since the early 400s AD.

30. Definition of Faith of the Council of Chalcedon (in Pelikan and Hotchkiss, *Creeds and Confessions*, 1:174–79); see Augsburg Confession item 3 (in Pelikan and Hotchkiss, *Creeds and Confessions*, 2:60); Church of England, Articles of Religion 2 (in Pelikan and Hotchkiss, *Creeds and Confessions*, 2:528); Westminster Confession of Faith 8:2 (in Pelikan and Hotchkiss, *Creeds and Confessions*, 2:616); Methodist Articles of Religion 2 (in Pelikan and Hotchkiss, *Creeds and Confessions*, 3:202); Church of the Nazarene Articles of Faith 2 (in Pelikan and Hotchkiss, *Creeds and Confessions*, 3:410).

31. The Lutheran Formula of Concord affirms the Blessed Virgin as "Mother of God" (in Pelikan and Hotchkiss, *Creeds and Confessions*, 2:191). Although the Church of England did not formally affirm this language, the Episcopal Church in the USA includes a portion of the Definition of Faith of the Council of Chalcedon in its *Book of Common Prayer* (1979), including its use of the term "God-bearer (Theotokos)"; in Episcopal Church, *Book of Common Prayer* (1979), 864. Reformed and Methodist churches have historically affirmed the Chalcedonian language of "one Person in two natures" (see the references in the previous note) but have not explicitly affirmed the use of terms like "God-bearer" or "Mother of God" to refer to the Blessed Virgin.

- A different group of Eastern churches we call "**Oriental Orthodox**" churches (not the same as "Eastern Orthodox" Churches) believe that the formula of Chalcedon does not sufficiently express the *unity* of the divine and human in Christ. They speak of "one nature" of Christ and they do refer to Mary as "God-bearer" or "Mother of God." Oriental Orthodox churches have been separate from other Christian communities since the mid-400s AD.

- After 1,500 years of division over these issues, ecumenical discussions in the twentieth century led to some **breakthrough agreements on these matters. In 1994, the Catholic Church** (represented by Pope John Paul II) **and the Assyrian Church of the East** (represented by its Catholicos [Patriarch] Mar Dinkha IV) **signed a "Common Christological Definition" that carefully laid out common understandings and affirmed each other's ways of speaking of the unity and integrity of divine and human in Christ**. The "Common Christological Definition" also recognized the appropriateness of the Assyrian Church's way of speaking of Mary as "the Mother of Christ our God and Savior" and the appropriateness of the Catholic Church's ways of speaking of Mary as "Mother of God" and "Mother of Christ."[32]

- Two years later, **Pope John Paul II signed a "Common Declaration" with the Catholicos (Patriarch) Karekin I of the Armenian Apostolic Church, one of the Oriental Orthodox Churches**. Like the "Common Christological Definition" with the Assyrian Church of the East, the agreement with the Armenian Catholicos expressed a wide ground of common teachings, utilizing some of the language of the Council of Chalcedon, and recognizing differences in languages and cultures between the churches that would account for some of the historic differences separating them. The agreement expressed the hope for further work towards unity between their churches.[33]

These debates and divisions over the unity of the divine and human in Jesus Christ were grounded in longstanding ways in which Christians had used particular words. They had sometimes presumed that what *they*

32. See "Common Christological Definition" in Pelikan and Hotchkiss, *Creeds and Confessions*, 3:852–55.

33. See "Common Declaration" in Pelikan and Hotchkiss, *Creeds and Confessions*, 3:867–70. This declaration resulted from a series of dialogues between the Catholic Church and Oriental Orthodox churches—see the documents given in Gros et al., *Growth in Agreement II*, 688–708.

meant by words like "nature" and "Person" were the same as what *other* people meant when they used these words. The resolutions they reached did not amount to ignoring the differences or simply declaring, "Can't we just be friends?" The resolutions relied on asking each other carefully what they meant when they used these words, listening carefully to each other, and then finding ways in which they could affirm what was meant even when they couldn't agree on a formula of words. What was at stake was the most central Christian teaching about God's own revelation in Jesus Christ.

The Gospel through the Year

Christian communities repeat the good news about Jesus Christ again and again as our most distinctive message. As Christian communities developed in the early centuries, they came to devote about a half of each year to the retelling of the gospel story. Christians had observed the Jewish festival of *Pesach* ("Passover") from the New Testament period (1 Cor 5:7–8) and perhaps other Jewish festivals, such as the "feast of weeks," which came to be called Pentecost by Greek-speaking Jews (Acts 20:16; 1 Cor 16:8).

Christian churches continued to celebrate Christ's death and resurrection in association with Passover, eventually settling on a Friday celebration of Christ's death and a Sunday celebration of Christ's resurrection in keeping with the days of the week on which those events were recorded in the Gospels. **A period of fasting in preparation for Easter evolved in the early centuries; this came to be called "the forty days"** (*quadragesima*; **"Lent" in English**). The forty-day fast of Lent recalled Jesus' own fasting in the wilderness, and it was typically observed from the time of waking up in the morning to sundown each day. Food was eaten after sundown.[34]

Another cluster of Christian celebrations focused on **the birth of Jesus**. Egyptian Christians from the 200s AD celebrated both the birth and the baptism of Jesus on January 6.[35] From the 300s AD, **Western churches began to observe December 25 as a separate day to celebrate Jesus' birth**, perhaps in response to the popular Roman feast of Saturnalia that in some perids had fallen on that calendar date. Christian communities generally

---

34. See Canons of the Council of Nicaea, no. 5, and the "Letter of the Synod of Nicaea to the Egyptians" in Tanner, *Decrees of the Ecumenical Councils*, 1:8, 19.

35. The Syriac text of the *Didascalia Apostolorum,* probably from the fourth century, states explicitly that Epiphany was observed on January 6; see *Didascalia Apostolorum* 3:8:6 (in Vööbus, *Didascalia Apostolorum in Syriac,* 38).

called this the festival of the nativity (birth) of Jesus, though in English it came to be called the "Christ Mass" or **Christmas**.[36] The celebration of Christ's birth spawned a period after Christmas to celebrate the revelation of Christ to the world, **the season of Theophany (the "appearing of God") or Epiphany ("revelation")**. Christian communities also came to observe a period before Christmas to celebrate the prophecies of the coming of Christ, **the season of Advent**.

By the 400s AD, the celebration of the Christian year had acquired a consistent form that told the Christian story in the life of Jesus:

- the season of **Advent**, celebrating the prophecies of Christ,

- the season of **Christmas**, celebrating Christ's birth,

- the season of **Epiphany or Theophany**, celebrating Christ's revelation to the world,

- the season of **Lent**, celebrating Christ's suffering and death, and

- the season of **Easter**, celebrating Christ's resurrection.

In addition to these celebrations of the life of Christ, Christian churches also observed the day of **Pentecost**, forty-nine days after Easter (fifty days, including Easter Day), celebrating the coming of the Holy Spirit and the birth of the Christian church.

Christian communities developed poetic and musical works to celebrate these gospel feasts. The following is a Latin poem chanted on Easter morning in Western churches:

VICTIMAE PASCHALI LAUDES
IMMOLENT CHRISTIANI
AGNUS REDEMIT OVES
CHRISTUS INNOCENS PATRI
RECONCILIAVIT PECCATORES

LET CHRISTIANS SING PRAISES
TO THE PASCHAL VICTIM
THE LAMB HAS REDEEMED THE SHEEP
CHRIST THE INNOCENT

36. An early instance of the date December 25 (*"viii kal. Ian."*) appears in a document entitled *Depositio Martirum* [*sic*] from the middle of the fourth century: in Mommsen, *Chronica Minora Saec.*, 72.

HAS RECONCILED SINNERS
TO THE FATHER

Sequence for Easter attributed to the German poet
and biographer Wipo, eleventh century AD[37]

The word "paschal" in this poem refers both to the Jewish celebration of Passover and the Christian celebration of Easter. The poem shows that Christ's death and resurrection were still understood in the context of the Jewish festival of Passover.

"Love Was His Meaning"

It makes a difference to tell the gospel story knowing that the one who "died for our sins according to the scriptures" was not a substitute for God or an agent of God or a messenger of God, but was actually God. In Christ, none other than God "emptied himself, taking the form of a slave . . . And being found in human form, he humbled himself, and became obedient to the point of death—even death on a cross" (Phil 2:7–8). What does the gospel mean? The English mystical writer Saint Julian of Norwich concluded her *Revelations of Divine Love* (AD 1413) with these reflections:

> You would know our Lord's meaning in this thing? Know it well.
> Love was his meaning. Who showed it to you? Love. What did he
> show you? Love. Why did he show it? For love. Hold on to this and
> you will know and understand love more and more. But you will
> not know or learn anything else—ever![38]

---

37. From the Easter sequence *Victimae paschali laudes*, "*De Sancto Sepulcro*," given in Blume, *Sequentiae Ineditae*, 27–28.

38. Julian of Norwich, *Revelations of Divine Love*, 212.

CHAPTER 3

Holy Bath

I WANT TO INVITE you to a deeper Christian faith. The gospel, the message about God's self-giving love in Jesus Christ, is the most distinctive message of the Christian faith and has been the consistent focus of Christian preaching and Christian worship. But how does one embrace the gospel and become a Christian? **The ritual entryway is the holy bath that Christians call baptism.** And yet the process of becoming a Christian involves more than simply the rite of baptism. It involves personal turning (conversion) to Christ, training in the Christian faith, profession of the faith, and often one's first communion in the Christian community.

The path of Christian initiation was itself initiated by Saint John the Baptist, an eccentric character who ate locusts and wild honey, wore a camel's-hair loincloth—that seems to have been about all he wore—and spent most of his time in wild outdoor places. Some religious leaders thought he was crazy, and not just because of what he ate and wore and didn't wear. John the Baptist was telling Jews that they needed to be immersed and purified, repenting of their sins. The fact that they were from good Jewish families, and that their ancestors had been through the waters of the Red Sea and the Jordan River, did not impress him at all. This is what he told them:

ΚΑΙ ΜΗ ΔΟΞΗΤΕ ΛΕΓΕΙΝ ΕΝ ΕΑΥΤΟΙC
ΠΑΤΕΡΑ ΕΧΟΜΕΝ ΤΟΝ ΑΒΡΑΑΜ
ΛΕΓω ΓΑΡ ΥΜΙΝ
ΟΤΙ ΔΥΝΑΤΑΙ Ο ΘΕΟC

ϵκ ΤϢΝ ΛΙΘϢΝ ΤΟΥΤϢΝ
ϵΓϵΙΡΔΙ ΤϵΚΝΔ ΤϢ ΔΒΡΔΔΜ

DO NOT PRESUME TO SAY AMONG YOURSELVES
WE HAVE ABRAHAM AS OUR FATHER
FOR I SAY TO YOU
THAT GOD IS ABLE FROM THESE STONES
TO RAISE UP CHILDREN FOR ABRAHAM

Matthew 3:9

Saint John made some sense in saying this. His point was that being righteous before God does not come from one's ancestors being Jews, from one's ancestors going through the water. **Being righteous is a decision each person must make.** So even those who have Jewish mothers need to become Jews in their hearts. Prophets loved to say stuff like that. Some Jews, like the historian Josephus, regarded John as a genuinely pious Jew. Others regarded him as a very disturbed person.

Christians understood John the Baptist to be the herald of Jesus, the one who went before Jesus to "prepare the way of the Lord" (Isa 40:3; Mark 1:3). Just as John's preaching and his practice of baptism inaugurated the ministry of Jesus, so the practice of baptism inaugurates the Christian life. John's ministry involved two elements that are crucial to beginning the Christian life: the need for a personal decision to turn to God, and the ritual of immersion in water.

Christian communities baptize and initiate people into the Christian faith in different ways, but there are certain **elements that almost all Christian communities practice** as they bring women and men into the fellowship of Christ.[1] These common practices include the following:

- **Conversion**—that is, repentance for sin and a decision to believe in Jesus Christ and to identify oneself with the Christian community;

- **Training** in the Christian faith;

---

1. World Council of Churches Faith and Order Commission, *Baptism, Eucharist and Ministry*, section on baptism, ¶¶ 1–23. Exceptions to the use of (water) baptism are the Salvation Army, which suspended the practices of baptism and the Lord's Supper, though it is not particularly opposed to them, and the Society of Friends (Quakers), who emphasize the spiritual nature of baptism and do not consider water to be necessary.

- **Profession** of the Christian faith in a congregation and the congregation's affirmation of the faith that the candidate professes;

- **Baptism** with water "in the name of the Father and of the Son and of the Holy Spirit," and often involving an anointing marking a person as being joined to Christ the Anointed One;

- Receiving **the Lord's Supper** in a Christian congregation for the first time.

Between different families of Christian churches, the order in which these elements occur varies considerably, but almost all Christian communities maintain these five practices in the process by which people are brought into the faith and into a Christian community. At the conclusion of this chapter, we'll consider the different ways in which these five elements of Christian initiation may be ordered, but first let's consider each of the elements.

Elements of Christian Initiation 1:
Conversion (Turning to Christ)

The book called the Acts of the Apostles tells a dramatic story about the early Christian disciples Paul and Silas and a jailer who held them in prison in Philippi. Paul and Silas had been locked up for disturbing the peace by their proclamation of the gospel. While they were praying and singing, an earthquake rattled the prison and opened its doors. The poor jailer, who was held personally responsible for them, presumed that his prisoners had escaped, and he contemplated committing suicide. Paul and Silas assured him that nobody had left. The story continues in the following words, recounting the actions of the jailer:

ΚΑΙ ΠΡΟΑΓΑΓωΝ ΑΥΤΟΥC ΕΞω ΕΦΗ
ΚΥΡΙΟΙ ΤΙ ΜΕ ΔΕΙ ΠΟΙΕΙΝ ΙΝΑ CωθΩ
ΟΙ ΔΕ ΕΙΠΑΝ
ΠΙCΤΕΥCΟΝ ΕΠΙ ΤΟΝ ΚΥΡΙΟΝ ΙΗCΟΥΝ
ΚΑΙ CωθΗCΗ CΥ ΚΑΙ Ο ΟΙΚΟC CΟΥ

AND BRINGING THEM OUTSIDE HE SAID
GENTLEMEN WHAT MUST I DO TO BE SAVED
AND THEY SAID TO HIM

BELIEVE IN THE LORD JESUS
AND YOU WILL BE SAVED
AND YOUR HOUSEHOLD

Acts 16:30–31

Paul and Silas then announced the gospel to the jailer's household, and "then he and his entire family were baptized without delay . . . and his entire family rejoiced that he had become a believer in God" (Acts 16:33–34). Paul himself had experienced a dramatic conversion, moving from his prior persecution of Christians to become the great advocate of the new faith (Acts 7:58–8:3; 9:1–31). Not all Christian conversions are so dramatic, but **becoming a Christian has to involve a decision to "believe in the Lord Jesus."**[2]

The word "conversion" comes from a Latin verb, *convertere*, that means "to turn around," as when a person turns around to go in a different direction. The word used in the Greek language of the New Testament literally means "to change one's mind" or one's thinking. It can also be translated as "repent." The Philippian jailer changed directions—changed his way of thinking—when he received the gospel. Paul changed directions—changed his mind—when he ceased persecuting Christians and became an advocate for Christ. To "believe in the Lord Jesus" means to turn away from whatever separates us from God and to turn towards Jesus Christ.

The word "believe" carries the meaning "to trust." This kind of believing is not simply an acknowledgment of facts; it involves heartfelt trust. The Reformation-age *Homilies* of the Church of England explain that the demons acknowledged Jesus to be "the Holy One of God" (Mark 1:24)—that is, they had the basic facts straight about who Jesus was. But the demons did not love or trust Jesus. So Christian faith has to involve more than the acknowledgment of the facts that Jesus is the Christ, the Lord, and God. The homily explained that **to "believe in the Lord Jesus" means to entrust ourselves to Jesus Christ**.[3] To "believe in the Lord Jesus" means that we begin to reciprocate the self-giving love that God has shown through Jesus Christ.

---

2. World Council of Churches Faith and Order Commission, *Baptism, Eucharist and Ministry*, section on baptism, ¶¶ 4, 8–10.

3. See homily "Of the Salvation of All Mankind," in Church of England, *Certain Sermons or Homilies*, 30.

Trust is a personal matter, and this act of trusting is intensely personal. It involves a relationship between each of us and Jesus Christ. It is also a family and a community matter. The Philippian jailer was told that if he would believe, he would be saved along with his whole household, so his whole household was baptized with him. Sometimes when we find it difficult to believe, our families and our church communities carry us through. They cannot believe for us, but they believe while we disbelieve, and they keep open the door for us to return to belief.[4]

One of the contributions of evangelical Christianity is its passionate insistence on the need for faith as a personal decision. "Do not presume to say among yourselves, 'We have Abraham for our father.'" Evangelicals have a folksy way of saying this, as I heard it: "Goin' to church don't no more make you a Christian than goin' to a garage makes you a' automobile." You're not a Christian because you go to church or because your parents or your grandparents were Christians. The evangelical critique was directed at state churches that had so presumed the Christian character of their nation that becoming a Christian simply involved nominal training in the faith, perhaps memorizing responses to a formal catechism, followed by the ritual of confirmation and then regular church attendance. Pietist and evangelical teachers—within and outside of state churches—insisted that becoming a Christian has to involve more than knowing facts and ritual words and actions.

The call for personal decision and personal faith is common to many religious traditions. I'd point to **a parallel with the Hindu religious tradition called *bhakti-marga***, "the way of devotion." Hindu communities, unlike Christian communities on this point, believe in a cycle of life, death, and rebirth (reincarnation). Hindu religious traditions offer ways to find "release" from this cycle. Older Hindu traditions taught the way of traditional sacrifices and ritual performance, ascetic practice and meditation, and careful performance of the duties appropriate to one's caste and one's station in life.

But the way of devotion maintained that simple acts of devotion (*bhakti*)—even apart from ritual sacrifice, meditative practices, or right actions—could lead immediately to "release," even for ordinary people.[5]

---

4. In comparison to this section of *A Deeper Christian Faith*, see the first paragraph of the section "Through the Holy Spirit" in Joint Commission of Churches in Turkey, *Christianity*, 21.

5. Hopkins, *Hindu Religious Tradition*, 90–95.

Consider these passages from the classic work of the *bhakti* tradition, the *Bhagavad Gītā*:

> A leaf, a flower, a fruit, or water,
>> Who presents to Me with devotion,
>
> That offering of devotion I
>> Accept from the devout-souled (giver).

> Even if a very evil doer
>> Reveres Me with single devotion,
>
> He must be regarded as righteous in spite of all;
>> For he has the right resolution. (*Bhagavad Gītā* 9:26, 30)[6]

Not surprisingly, *bhakti-marga* gained great popularity among ordinary folk as their way of practicing Hinduism. *The Bhagavad Gita* makes explicit the claim that ordinary people can attain release by devotion:

> For if they take refuge in me, son of Pṛthā,
>> Even those who may be of base origin,
>
> Women, men of the artisan caste, and serfs too,
>> Even they go to the highest goal! (*Bhagavad Gītā* 9:32)[7]

Christianity and Hinduism are very different, but on the specific matter of the need for personal devotion or conversion (turning) of the soul, there is a parallel between Christian religious life and this Hindu spiritual tradition. Like the Hindu tradition of *bhakti-marga*, Christian conversion has a democratic ethos. It doesn't require sophisticated religious learning, ascetic practice, meditative discipline, or proper ritual performance. **It simply requires a heart that turns to God in Jesus Christ: "Believe in the Lord Jesus."**

Elements of Christian Initiation 2: Training in the Faith

Although evangelical teachers criticized churches that only gave instruction in the faith and then a ritual confirmation, **initiation in the Christian faith does need to involve training, instruction, or formation in the Christian faith and Christian practices**. Consider the following verse from the letter to the Ephesians:

---

6. Edgerton, *Bhagavad Gītā*, 48 and 49.

7. Edgerton, *Bhagavad Gītā*, 49.

ΚΑΙ ΟΙ ΠΑΤΕΡΕC
ΜΗ ΠΑΡΟΡΓΙΖΕΤΕ ΤΑ ΤΕΚΝΑ ΥΜΩΝ
ΑΛΛΑ ΕΚΤΡΕΦΕΤΕ ΑΥΤΑ
ΕΝ ΠΑΙΔΕΙΑ ΚΑΙ ΝΟΥΘΕCΙΑ ΚΥΡΙΟΥ

AND FATHERS
DO NOT MAKE YOUR CHILDREN ANGRY
BUT NURTURE THEM
IN THE TRAINING AND ADMONITION
OF THE LORD

Ephesians 6:4

This exhortation appears in a code of family conduct with instructions for mothers, fathers, children, and servants. Two key words that appear in the exhortation to fathers are "training" and "admonition." The word "training" can also be translated "upbringing," "training," "instruction," or "discipline." Similarly, the word "admonition" can also be translated as "admonition," "instruction," or "discipline." The two words have overlapping meanings, and they imply that fathers should engage themselves in the guidance or formation of their children in ways that involve more than simply teaching facts or doctrines. Early Christian instruction in the faith, for new candidates for baptism as well as the children of believers, involved just such a program of moral, spiritual, and doctrinal formation.

The term that eventually prevailed in churches for the practice of Christian formation and instruction was from a verb that means "to sound down," that is, to sound in the ears of hearers. The words "**catechesis**" (instruction in the faith) and "**catechism**" (a specific form of instruction in the faith) are derived from this word. Catechesis was at first an oral practice: a teacher or "catechist" sounded the words that were heard by learners or "catechumens," who memorized the words they heard. **This book is itself structured as a re-sounding or re-catechism** for those who want a deeper and renewed sense of the historic Christian faith.

As Christian catechesis took a more consistent shape in the Latin-speaking (Western) church in the Middle Ages, it typically involved the following items to be learned by catechumens:

- **The Apostles' Creed** as the basic statement of Christian faith to be professed at baptism or confirmation,

- **The Lord's Prayer** as a basic form of prayer for Christians,

- **The Great Commandments** (to love God and one's neighbor) **and the Ten Commandments** as the bases of Christian morality, and

- Instruction about the Christian **sacraments**.

After the age of the reformations, Protestant catechisms adopted this general outline of contents. Martin Luther's *Small Catechism* (1529), for example, utilized the same outline. The first edition of John Calvin's extensive, systematic exposition of Christian beliefs, the *Institutes of the Christian Religion* (1536), utilized the same general outline but expanded it, adding a section on church governance. This book includes all of these elements—i.e., the creeds (chapters 1–2), the Lord's Prayer, the commandments (chapter 6), and instruction about the sacraments (chapters 3–4). Texts of the Lord's Prayer, the Apostles' Creed, the Nicene Creed, and a summary of the Commandments are given in an appendix to this book.

Christian communities in the West developed formal printed catechisms for the instruction of candidates. Each of the major Western Christian traditions at the time of the reformations developed its own catechism:

- The *Catechism of the Council of Trent* for the Catholic Church, replaced in recent decades by *The Catechism of the Catholic Church* (1992);

- The *Luther Small Catechism* for Lutheran churches;

- The *Westminster Shorter Catechism* for Presbyterian churches;

- The *Heidelberg Catechism* for German Reformed and some other Reformed churches; and

- The catechism of the *Book of Common Prayer* (revised a number of times) for Anglicans.

Each of these contained instruction on the basic content of Christian faith, usually following the text of the Apostles' Creed, instruction in Christian morality, instruction in Christian spirituality (especially prayer), and instruction on the sacraments.

The catechisms from the Middle Ages and the period of the reformations don't have **instruction in the Christian Scriptures**. There's a reason for that. The reformations occurred hand-in-hand with the spread of literacy in Western Europe, following the invention of the modern printing press in the 1450s. As printing and literacy became more widespread, Bibles became more and more available to ordinary people. The Catholic Church and Protestant churches alike sponsored translations of the Bible in vernacular languages. The result has been that biblical learning has become a critical element of Christian formation since that time. However, Christian communities do not typically expect candidates for baptism and profession of the faith to be deeply formed in the Scriptures, so extensive training in the Scriptures tends to come as part of the believer's ongoing formation beyond their initial catechesis in the Christian faith.

Elements of Christian Initiation 3: Profession of the Faith

A central part of the process of Christian initiation is profession of the Christian faith on the part of a candidate.[8] We have seen Saint Augustine's reference to the practice of the Roman congregation in his age of candidates for baptism professing their faith from a raised platform "in a set form of words" they had memorized.

Another way for candidates to profess their faith was by way of **answers to questions set for them by church leaders**. An ancient Christian document that illustrates this practice is called *The Apostolic Tradition*. This document is believed to reflect the practice of the Roman community in the 200s AD, almost two hundred years before the time that Augustine described. The document exists in a variety of manuscripts and languages, with many textual variations. A Western, Latin variation of the text gives a description of the process of examination of candidates for baptism. The one performing the baptism asked three main questions, and they begin like this:

CREDIS IN DEUM
PATREM OMNIPOTENTEM

DO YOU BELIEVE IN GOD
THE FATHER ALL-POWERFUL

CREDIS IN IESUM CHRISTUM
FILIUM DEI

DO YOU BELIEVE IN JESUS CHRIST
THE SON OF GOD

8. See the section on baptism in World Council of Churches Faith and Order Commission, *Baptism, Eucharist and Ministry*, ¶ 20.

CREDIS IN SPIRITU SANCTO

DO YOU BELIEVE IN THE HOLY SPIRIT

Latin recension of The Apostolic Tradition[9]

These are only the beginnings of the three questions. The full text of the questions contains more creedal material like that of the Apostles' Creed. According to this Western text of *The Apostolic Tradition*, **the candidate would say** *credo*, **"I believe," in response to each of these questions,** and at each response, the candidate was "baptized" or immersed. So the profession followed this order.

- The celebrant asked the candidate about the first part of the Creed, beginning with, "Do you believe in God the Father almighty?" The candidate responded, "I believe," and the candidate was immersed the first time.

- The celebrant asked the candidate about their belief in Jesus Christ, beginning with, "Do you believe in Jesus Christ the Son of God?" The candidate responded, "I believe," and the candidate was immersed the second time.

- The celebrant asked the candidate about their belief in the Holy Spirit, beginning with, "Do you believe in the Holy Spirit?" The candidate responded, "I believe," and the candidate was immersed the third time.

The three immersions thus followed the Trinitarian ordering of the creed, dramatizing the candidate's baptism "in the name of the Father, and of the Son, and of the Holy Spirit."

In Eastern Christian churches, profession of the faith comes with a renunciation of Satan and then the affirmation of the Christian faith in the words of the Nicene Creed. The Latin-speaking Western church in the Middle Ages began to associate training in the faith (catechesis) and profession of the faith with the separate rite of confirmation. Following this pattern, profession in the Catholic Church also involved the formal renunciations of sin and the devil. Catechesis and profession were thus separated from baptism and postponed until candidates could learn the faith and profess it on their own.

---

9. In *The Apostolic Tradition*, 84 and 86. The translation is my own.

The previous section has mentioned the historic catechisms used by Western Christians. Part of the service of profession in these churches is an examination of candidates by a celebrant who asks candidates questions from the catechism. This process of asking questions based on a more detailed catechism could be interpreted as candidates being asked to affirm all of the content of the catechism at the time of their confirmation or profession. Conservative folks within each of these church traditions have understood the examination of candidates in this way. But in almost all cases, the way these questions were stated was not "Do you believe," etc. Rather, it was simply a matter of checking to see if candidates knew and could state the teachings of their church. **What they were asked to affirm for themselves was a much smaller cluster of common beliefs professed using the words of the Apostles' Creed.** That is to say, candidates were not asked to affirm the teachings of their church in detail: they were required to demonstrate that they *knew* the teachings of their church before they professed the Christian faith and were formally received into their church.

In recent decades, Anglican churches, many Protestant churches, and the Catholic Church have revised their rites of profession to include renunciations of evil and affirmation of the Christian faith in a question-and-answer form of profession like those of *The Apostolic Tradition*. Candidates renounce evil in response to a series of questions, for example (from the Episcopal *Book of Common Prayer*), "Do you renounce Satan and all the spiritual forces of wickedness that rebel against God?" The candidate responds to each question, "I renounce them." Candidates then affirm the Christian faith in response to three questions: "Do you believe in God the Father?" "Do you believe in Jesus Christ, the Son of God?" "Do you believe in God the Holy Spirit?" The candidate responds by reciting, with the congregation, each of the three articles of the Apostles' Creed. Candidates are then asked a series of questions about their commitments for future action: for example, "Will you strive for justice and peace among all people, and respect the dignity of every human being?" The candidate responds to each of these questions, "I will, with God's help."[10]

These are not wussy renunciations or affirmations. They call for sincere repentance and conversion, they name the faith in the words of the ancient creed, and they make specific commitments in the presence of a

---

10. Quotations and summaries from the profession in the rite of baptism are from the 1979 Prayer Book of the Episcopal Church (USA) (Episcopal Church, *Book of Common Prayer*, 302–5).

congregation that witnesses their promises. **The revision of the baptismal profession on the part of older Protestant churches has thus become a point of renewal, strengthening commitments to historic Christian beliefs and practices.**

Elements of Christian Initiation 4: Baptism and Anointing

Baptism itself is the almost-universal practice by which candidates are received into Christian communities. There are only a few exceptions. Friends or Quakers have historically maintained that they do indeed believe in the baptism of the Holy Spirit, but that the outward sign of water is not particularly necessary for Christians. The Salvation Army does not practice baptism, but on the other hand has never formally rejected or criticized the practice. The Salvation Army simply made a decision early in its history to suspend the practices of baptism and the Lord's Supper. There may be other exceptions like these, but it is a point of remarkable unity across the range of Christian communities that they practice baptism as the means appointed by Christ by which persons are brought into the Christian community.

The practice of baptism is grounded in the words of Jesus recorded in the Gospel according to Matthew:

ΠΟΡΕΥΘΕΝΤΕС ΟΥΝ
ΜΑΘΗΤΕΥСΑΤΕ ΠΑΝΤΑ ΤΑ ΕΘΝΗ
ΒΑΠΤΙΖΟΝΤΕС ΑΥΤΟΥС ΕΙС ΤΟ ΟΝΟΜΑ
ΤΟΥ ΠΑΤΡΟС
ΚΑΙ ΤΟΥ ΥΙΟΥ
ΚΑΙ ΤΟΥ ΑΓΙΟΥ ΠΝΕΥΜΑΤΟС
ΔΙΔΑСΚΟΝΤΕС ΑΥΤΟΥС
ΤΗΡΕΙΝ ΠΑΝΤΑ ΟСΑ ΕΝΕΤΕΙΛΑΜΗΝ ΥΜΙΝ

GOING THEREFORE
DISCIPLE ALL THE NATIONS
BAPTIZING THEM IN THE NAME
OF THE FATHER
AND OF THE SON
AND OF THE HOLY SPIRIT

TEACHING THEM TO OBSERVE
ALL THAT I HAVE COMMANDED YOU

Matthew 28:19–20

The word conventionally translated "make disciples" actually says nothing about "making." The word used in this verse is a verb based on the noun "disciple," so I have made it into a verb (an awkward one) in the translation here. The point is that Christian communities are to be involved in forming people as disciples of Jesus Christ. They are to form people as disciples, "baptizing them in the name of the Father, and of the Son, and of the Holy Spirit," and the traditional Christian baptismal formula, "I baptize you in the name of the Father, and of the Son, and of the Holy Spirit" is based directly on this passage.

The word "baptizing" in this passage from Matthew **literally means "dunking" or "immersing."** Christians in desert climates where water is scarce, and in northern climates where they were concerned for the health of people to be baptized in frigid water, began to pour water or even to sprinkle water on candidates as an alternative to full immersion. Eastern Christians continued to practice immersion, but pouring or sprinkling became the norm in the West. Most unfortunately, sprinkling became associated with casual, mass baptisms in the Middle Ages.

Historians are almost unanimously agreed that immersion was the normative mode of baptism in early Christian churches, and ecumenical discussions of baptism have privileged immersion as a preferred mode of baptism.[11] It is also the case that early Christians were not terribly worried about the quantity of water used in baptism. The following passage is from an early Christian document called the *Didache* or "Teaching of the Twelve Disciples," usually dated from the second century AD:

> Now concerning baptism, baptize as follows: after you have re-
> viewed all these things [Christian training or catechesis], baptize
> in the name of the Father and of the Son and of the Holy Spirit in
> running water. But if you have no running water, then baptize in
> some other water; and if you are not able to baptize in cold water,
> then do so in warm. But if you have neither, then pour water on

---

11. See the section on baptism in World Council of Churches Faith and Order Commission, *Baptism, Eucharist and Ministry,* ¶ 18.

the head three times in the name of the Father and of the Son and of the Holy Spirit.[12]

This passage suggests that alternatives to full immersion were allowed, but it also makes it clear that immersion was the preferred mode of baptism.

Liturgical reforms in Western Christian churches in recent decades have led them to work towards embracing immersion as a preferred mode of baptism. The Catholic Church urges strongly against sprinkling, given the historical connotations of this way of baptizing, and Protestant as well as Catholic churches in recent decades have begun to build immersion baptisteries so that immersion can become a customary practice.

Did the earliest Christians baptize infants? The New Testament records baptisms of whole families (Acts 16:15 and 33), although these verses do not indicate if the families included infants, or if any were excluded because of their age. There can be little doubt that in the earliest decades, baptisms were overwhelmingly of mature (adult) believers. The evidence from later centuries (from the late 100s on) is mixed: some communities decided to baptize children of believers, others did not. Eventually, the practice of baptizing infant children of believers prevailed, though we will see that many Christian communities that baptize infants today have come to regard adult baptism with mature profession of faith as a theological norm, if not the most widespread practice.[13] Anabaptist and Baptist churches baptize believers only and do not baptize infants.

The most historic Christian communities—Orthodox, Catholic, and Anglican churches—associate baptism with **anointing**. The connection with anointing for Christians may not be obvious, but the words "Christ" and "Christian" are derived from a word that means "to anoint." Anointing with oil was a very common ancient practice understood as a sign that identified a person as a follower of Christ, the "anointed one." Anointing was also associated with cleansing (oil was used as a cleansing agent) and with healing, and these meanings were also associated with baptism.

A distinct practice in historic Christian churches is to baptize a person, **calling their name without a surname**—that is, they are baptized only with their first and middle names, their "Christian names" (baptismal names). This dates from the time before surnames became common, from

12. *Didache* 7:1–3 from the edition and translation of Michael W. Holmes, *Apostolic Fathers*, 354 (text) and 355 (translation).

13. See the section on baptism in World Council of Churches Faith and Order Commission, *Baptism, Eucharist and Ministry*, ¶ 11.

the 1200s AD in Western Europe. I do not actually know what custom the pastor who baptized me followed, but if he had followed the older custom, he would have said, "Ted Allen, I baptize thee in the name of the Father, and of the Son, and of the Holy Spirit."[14] Traditional Christian services of ordination and marriage used only baptismal names, and many Christians in India have taken "Christian" as their surname, indicating that they have taken the Christian community as their larger family.

Christian baptisms are generally acknowledged across denominational boundaries, even across the boundaries of churches that do not share the Lord's Supper with each other. Eastern Orthodox church law technically does not allow the recognition of baptisms performed outside of Orthodox churches, although, by a principle of practical application, many Orthodox churches today do not rebaptize when receiving Christians from other church communions. Churches that do not baptize infants typically do not acknowledge infant baptisms performed by other churches, and require baptism upon entering their communities. In doing this, they do not consider their practice to be rebaptism, because they do not acknowledge the prior act considered to be "baptism" in other churches.

This raises the issue of **what constitutes a valid baptism**. The Catholic Church has three requirements for recognizing a baptism:

- **water** must be used,

- the baptism must be performed **in the name of the Father and of the Son and of the Holy Spirit,** and

- the one performing the baptism must have **the intention to do what the church does in baptism.**[15]

This last expression means that, for example, if a non-Christian actor is "baptized" by another actor in a play using water, "in the name of the Father and of the Son and of the Holy Spirit," the act would still not be recognized as a baptism because, in the play, the actors did not *intend* to do what Christian communities do in baptism.[16]

---

14. He may have said "you" in place of "thee," and many Methodist pastors by this time had begun to follow the modern custom of including surnames in baptism.

15. Catholic Church, "Directory for the Application of Principles," para. 93.

16. In comparison to this section of *A Deeper Christian Faith*, see the section "One Baptism and Repentance for the Forgiveness of Our Sins" in Joint Commission of Churches in Turkey, *Christianity*, 64–66.

Elements of Christian Initiation 5: First Communion

In many Christian communities, **a candidate's first time receiving the Lord's Supper (first communion) is an important part of the process of initiation into the Christian faith.** The Supper will be the subject of the next chapter, but we can observe here that a variety of patterns have emerged for receiving one's first communion as part of the process of Christian initiation. In Eastern Christian churches, infants are chrismated (anointed) and baptized and then given their first communion within the space of Saturday evening and Sunday morning, sometimes even within one service. The Catholic Church in the West separated baptism from catechesis and confirmation, and the custom evolved in the Roman Church in the Middle Ages that children received their first communion around eight years of age, a few years before they undergo catechesis and confirmation. This was partly due to the fear that younger children might treat the elements of the communion service without appropriate reverence.

Protestant churches until quite recently reserved communion until the time of confirmation, and in this way it was connected directly to the process of initiation. Although this practice continues in some churches, many older Protestant communities (Anglican, Lutheran, Presbyterian, Congregational, and Methodist churches) now encourage children to receive communion soon after baptism. Churches that practice believers' baptism reserve the Lord's Supper until a person has had a conversion experience and has made a profession of their faith. Receiving communion for the first time is simply seen as part of their ongoing life in the community, not a moment in the process of Christian initiation. As we will see in the next chapter, the Lord's Supper has been understood as the fullest sign of belonging to a Christian community, so it is important that newly baptized Christians participate in the Lord's Supper to indicate their inclusion in a particular Christian community.

Patterns of Christian Initiation

Most Christian communities insist on each of these elements of Christian initiation: a personal decision to turn (convert) to Christ, training in the faith (catechesis), personal profession of the faith, and the rite of baptism itself, sometimes accompanied by anointing and sometimes followed by first communion. But in the varied Christian communities, these elements of Christian initiation are likely to follow different patterns.

- In **Eastern Christian churches**, including Eastern Orthodox and Oriental Orthodox churches, the typical pattern of initiation involves infant baptism (by immersion), accompanied by anointings, one of which is the great anointing referred to as chrismation. This is followed by the infant's first communion, usually within a day of the infant's baptism. Training in the faith and public profession come later in a young person's life.

- The pattern of Christian initiation that has prevailed in the **Catholic Church and in older Protestant churches** involves infant baptism, followed by first communion (for Catholics), followed by training in the faith and confirmation, at which point a young person makes their public profession of Christian faith. For older Protestant churches, first communion might follow confirmation (the older pattern) or might come soon after baptism (the more contemporary pattern). Of course, adults are also candidates for baptism in the Catholic Church, in older Protestant churches, and in Eastern Christian churches as well, and in these cases the order would be different with training in the faith coming before baptism and profession.

- A third pattern of Christian initiation is typical of **evangelical churches** and it involves a mature decision to follow Christ, followed by personal profession of the faith and baptism, followed by training in the faith. First communion typically does not play a significant role in this pattern.

In recent decades, influenced by the ecumenical movement and especially the common movement for liturgical renewal, the Catholic Church and older Protestant churches have come to affirm that **baptism accompanied by a mature profession of the Christian faith should be seen as a normative practice**. This point of view is reflected in the World Council of Churches' consensus document entitled *Baptism, Eucharist and Ministry* (1983), which states that "baptism upon personal profession of faith is the most clearly attested pattern in the New Testament documents."[17]

17. World Council of Churches Faith and Order Commission, *Baptism, Eucharist and Ministry*, 4.

A sign of the prevalence of this view is the Catholic Church's develop-ment of the *Rite of Christian Initiation for Adults,* which entails not only a ritual but also an extensive program of formation in Christian faith.[18] In many older Protestant churches, a ritual for adult baptism is now placed first in service books and hymnals, with a rite of baptism for infants and others who cannot answer for themselves taking second place. This reverses the order in which these rituals had appeared in traditional service books and hymnals, and it indicates a growing sense of the normative character of adult baptism.

This does not mean that the churches that historically baptize infants will cease doing so in the near future. It might mean that they become more open to postponing baptism in many cases, and encouraging confirmation when young people make decisions on their own to learn about and profess the Christian faith, rather than expecting all of a certain age to make their profession together.

Baptism is the entryway to the Christian faith. It is the nearly uni-versal rite, instituted by Christ himself, by which Christian communities bring people into their fellowship. But baptism is only part of a rich process of initiation into the Christian faith. It has to be joined by a sincere decision to believe in and follow Christ, training in the faith, public profession of the faith, and a candidate's participation in the Supper of the Lord, the subject of the next chapter. In baptism we die and rise with Christ (Rom 6:3–4). We die to our old selves and rise with Christ to a new life. As Christ's life and death were his offering for us, our death to sin and our new life in Christ following baptism begin our giving up of ourselves for God and for others.

---

18. The normative nature of adult baptism is expressed in *The Catechism of the Catho-lic Church* (¶¶ 1229–33), which describes the elaborate catechumenate of the ancient church including mature baptism, and contrasts this with infant baptism as only "the preparatory stages of Christian initiation in a very abridged way" (¶ 1231) whereas the adult catechumenate (with adult baptism) involves all of the stages in their fullest expression.

CHAPTER 4

Holy Feast

I WANT TO INVITE you to a deeper Christian faith. The Christian gospel is the message about God's self-giving love in Jesus Christ, and baptism is the act by which Christian communities bring women and men into the life of self-giving love. Believers hear the gospel and profess it, and they move from the waters of baptism to the fermented wine and bread of the Supper. They move into a life of self-giving love through **the holy feast that Saint Paul called "the Lord's Supper"** (1 Cor 11:20).

Catholics came to call the feast the **"Mass,"** from the Latin term for the dismissal (*missa*) at the conclusion of the service. Eastern Orthodox Christians call it the **"Divine Liturgy,"** and Aramaic-speaking Christian communities, such as the Syriac Orthodox Church, the Assyrian Church of the East, and the Mar Thoma Church of India, call it the **"Sacred Qurbana,"** from the Aramaic word for "gift" (a word used in Mark 7:11). It is often called **"holy communion"** in Protestant churches. The term **"Eucharist"** has been frequently used in Catholic and ecumenical circles, from the biblical Greek word for "thanksgiving" (the root word is in 1 Corinthians 11:24 and Luke 17:19).

The Acts of the Apostles gives a little glimpse of the life of early Christian communities:

ЄN ΔЄ TH MIΔ TⲰN CΔBBΔTⲰN
CYNHΓMЄNⲰN HMⲰN
KⲖΔCΔI ΔPTON

WHEN WE MET
ON THE FIRST DAY OF THE WEEK
TO BREAK BREAD

Acts 20:7

This passage describes "the breaking of bread" (see Acts 2:42 also) as the ordinary practice of Christians on the first day of the week. This probably denoted a fellowship meal as well as the sacred celebration of the offering of Christ (see the section below on "Fasting and Feasting"). For fifteen centuries, the weekly worship of Christian communities on "the Lord's Day" (Rev 1:10) focused on the Lord's Supper, and even today **the central Sunday worship service for most Christian communities involves the Lord's Supper.**[1]

Many Protestant communities since the 1500s have offered forms of Sunday worship, such as preaching services, that do not always involve the Lord's Supper. Most Protestant churches do celebrate the Supper regularly and have worked to increase the regularity of Christians receiving the Supper. Some American Protestant groups, in fact, such as Churches of Christ and Disciples of Christ, insist on the weekly celebration of the Supper, following the practice of the primitive church, often citing Acts 20:7 as their explicit New Testament basis.

But other Protestant groups—especially those identified as "evangelical" Protestant communities—have Sunday-morning activities that are structured more as evangelistic events designed for people who have not been part of Christian communities in the past or who have held only a nominal Christian faith. These events typically do not involve the Supper.

In this chapter, we are concerned with the holy feast that has been the typical form of worship for Christian communities since New Testament times, the feast that celebrates the mystery of the self-giving love of God in Jesus Christ. Saint Paul claimed that, "as often as you eat this bread and drink the cup, you proclaim the Lord's death until he comes" (1 Cor 11:26). **The holy feast is the most complete unfolding of the work of Jesus**

---

1. Catholic, Eastern Orthodox, Oriental Orthodox, Assyrian Church of the East, Churches of Christ, Disciples of Christ, and many Lutheran and Anglican communities celebrate the Supper every Sunday. Catholics are themselves the statistical majority of Christians in the world today, accounting for more than 50 percent (more than a billion) of the total number of Christians (over two billion) in the world.

Christ. But the meaning of the holy feast is tied up with ancient and almost forgotten meanings.

Fasting and Feasting

The ancestors of my Campbell family are accused of murdering a group of fellow Scots of Clan Donald in 1692. The story, as it has been elaborated through the centuries, depicts the Campbells as inviting the MacDonalds to an elaborate dinner, plying them with liquor, then butchering them in their sleep. This would have been regarded as a horrifying act, not only because of the murders, but because murder following a meal together violated the ancient understanding that a meal signifies fellowship and reconciliation.

One of the most basic meanings of the Lord's Supper is the notion of a feast together as a sign of reconciliation and fellowship,[2] and not just a feast with fellow humans, but one where God is also present. There is more than that: ancient feasts were often associated with offerings to God, and the Lord's Supper cannot be deeply understood apart from its meaning as an offering. But the Supper grew out of a Christian practice of feasting.

The Christian life does not require an endless diet of bologna sandwiches. It is a life of fasting and of feasting. As early Christian communities came to regularize their life together, they took up the custom of fasting on Wednesdays and Fridays from waking until midafternoon. They observed Sunday as a feast day, "the Lord's Day" (Rev 1:10; see also Acts 20:7; 1 Cor 16:2), the day of the resurrection. They also began to observe feasts to commemorate saints and martyrs, typically on the date of a saint's or martyr's death. They came to observe the season of Lent as a time of fasting, typically from waking up until sunset, but they interrupted the great fast of Lent to observe Sundays as feast days in conjunction with the Lord's Supper.

Shared meals have been part of the Christian experience since the very beginning. Here's how the Acts of the Apostles depicts the Christian community in the first days of its existence:

HCAN ΔE ΠΡΟCΚΑΡΤΕΡΟΥΝΤΕC
ΤΗ ΔΙΔΑΧΗ ΤΩΝ ΑΠΟCΤΟΛΩΝ
ΚΑΙ ΤΗ ΚΟΙΝΩΝΙΑ

2. See the section on Eucharist in World Council of Churches Faith and Order Commission, *Baptism, Eucharist and Ministry*, ¶ 1. See also Bradshaw, *Reconstructing Early Christian Worship*, 3–19; and Sumney, *Steward of God's Mysteries*, 142–56.

ΤΗ ΚΛΛCΕΙ ΤΟΥ ΛΡΤΟΥ
ΚΛΙ ΤΛΙC ΠΡΟCΕΥΧΛΙC

THEY DEVOTED THEMSELVES
TO THE APOSTLES TEACHING
AND FELLOWSHIP
TO THE BREAKING OF BREAD
AND THE PRAYERS

Acts 2:42

"The apostles' teaching" probably refers to the content of the gospel that Saint Peter had announced in the verses preceding. "Fellowship" might mean simply hanging around together, although the word can also imply sharing goods together, as the early Christian community did (Acts 2:44–45). "The prayers" might refer to traditional Jewish prayers said at specific hours of the day, as other verses in the Acts of the Apostles indicate (Acts 2:15; 3:1; 10:9; and 10:30). "The breaking of bread" suggests a common meal related to the Lord's Supper.

There is no distinction made in this passage from the Acts between the Supper as a sacred rite and the Supper as a shared meal, but such a distinction had to be made by the time of Saint Paul. In fact, Paul himself may have been the one who began to make the distinction.[3] Paul was aware that some members of the Corinthian community came into the assembly and proceeded to eat a meal they had brought, while others had nothing to eat (1 Cor 11:20–22). His advice was that if people were really hungry, they should eat at home (11:33–34). Following his instructions, the Supper itself was not primarily for the purpose of feasting, but was a sacred rite accompanied by eating bread and drinking wine together.

Despite the distinction that Saint Paul made, **the New Testament and early Christian literature give evidence that meals continued to be shared by Christian communities.**[4] Chapter 6 of the Acts of the Apostles speaks of the "daily distribution of food" (Acts 6:1), and Acts 20:7 and 11 speak again of the "breaking of bread." Verse 12 of the letter of Jude and some manuscripts of 2 Peter 2:13 refer to inappropriate conduct associated with meals they called "love feasts." A letter of Saint Ignatius of Antioch to the Smyrnaeans, dating from around AD 115, stipulated that a love feast

3. Bradshaw, *Reconstructing Early Christian Worship*, 18–19.
4. Young, *Sacrifice and the Death of Christ*, 62–63.

should not be held apart from the bishop.[5] Around AD 200, the African writer Tertullian described Sunday evening meals shared by Christians.[6] The meals Tertullian described seem to be the same as the love feasts described earlier. Even today, blessed but unconsecrated bread is shared at the conclusion of the Divine Liturgy in Eastern Orthodox churches, a little reminder of the early Christian love feast. Moravians and Methodists would revive the practice of the love feast in the eighteenth century.

The Lord's Supper, then, grew out of a common meal that signifies fellowship and reconciliation. When I greeted my friend Gary MacDonald at the Supper for many years, I would say, "Peace to you and to the House of Donald." Gary replied, "And to you, and your kin loyal to Argyll." He was offering peace to the Campbells.[7] We need it.

The Tradition of the Supper

In the first letter to the Corinthians, Saint Paul transmitted the earliest words recorded about the Lord's Supper. He began these words with a formula of tradition parallel to those in 1 Corinthians 15:1 and 3:

ϵΓⲰ ΓⲀⲢ ΠⲀⲢϵⲗⲗⲂⲞⲚ
ⲀΠⲞ ϮⲞⲨ ⲔⲨⲢⲒⲞⲨ
Ⲟ ⲔⲀⲒ ΠⲀⲢϵⲗⲰⲔⲀ ⲨⲘⲒⲚ

FOR I RECEIVED FROM THE LORD
THAT WHICH I HANDED ON TO YOU

1 Corinthians 11:23

Like the parallel passage in 1 Corinthians 15:1 and 3, Paul used the technical vocabulary associated with the oral "receiving" (hearing) and "handing on" (reciting) a set form of words. The claim that these words

5. See Ignatius of Antioch's Letter to the Smyrnaeans 8:2 in the translation of Holmes, *Apostolic Fathers*, 256 (text) and 257 (translation).

6. Tertullian, *Apol.* 39:16–18; a translation is given in McKinnon, *Music in Early Christian Literature*, 43 (item 74) and is referenced in essay 8, "On the Question of Psalmody in the Ancient Synagogue," in McKinnon's *Temple, the Church Fathers*, 95–96.

7. Gary Bruce MacDonald reflected on our greetings in an article entitled "By Faith By Hope," originally published in the journal of Clan Donald (USA), *By Sea By Land* (Winter 2014). This was subsequently republished (at my urging) in the *Journal of the Clan Campbell Society of North America*.

are "from the Lord" has led some interpreters to suppose that Saint Paul received these words by a direct revelation from Jesus Christ, but, embedded in a formula of oral tradition, they more likely mean that he "received" the form of words from Christ through those who had heard it and handed it on to others.

The use of a formula of tradition means that these words, like the tradition of the gospel in 1 Corinthians 15, comprise **one of the very oldest texts we have about Jesus.** If Paul was writing in the decade of the 50s AD, then his claim to have "received" these words earlier places them in an earlier decade, within twenty-five years of the events they describe. The fact that the Supper is one of these oldest elements of Christian tradition points to the importance it had in the earliest Christian communities.

The Lord's Supper as Participation in Christ's Offering

The Supper and its meaning pointing to Christ's life, death, and resurrection were bound up in the minds of early Christians with ancient practices of making offerings to gods.[8] The practice of making offerings was familiar to ancient people. When they heard words associated with offerings and sacrifices, their minds were filled with sights, smells, sounds, tastes, and textures associated with them. These practices are alien to most modern people, so when we hear words associated with offerings and sacrifices, we are likely to envision meanings only loosely related to the ancient practices of offerings and sacrifices: "offering," for example, might conjure up images of collection plates being distributed at church. The meanings we're likely to associate with these words are far removed from their ancient contexts, so for us to grasp the meaning of the Supper and the deeper meanings of the work of Christ embedded in it, we need to call to mind some things that have been long forgotten.[9]

Let's try leaving some of the words about offerings untranslated. Consider this passage in Paul's letter to the Romans:

8. World Council of Churches Faith and Order Commission, *Baptism, Eucharist and Ministry*, section on eucharist, ¶ 8; see additionally the commentary attached to ¶ 8.

9. In comparison to this section of *A Deeper Christian Faith*, see the sections "The Sacrificial System," "The Inadequacy of the Sacrificial Animal," and "Jesus Christ: The True Sacrifice" in Joint Commission of Churches in Turkey, *Christianity*, 41–45.

ΔΙΚΛΙΟΥΜΕΝΟΙ ΔШΡΕΛΝ ΤΗ ΛΥΤΟΥ ΧΛΡΙΤΙ
ΔΙΛ ΤΗС ΛΠΟΛΥΤΡШСΕШС
ΤΗС ΕΝ ΧΡΙСΤШ ΙΗСΟΥ
ΟΝ ΠΡΟΕΘΕΤΟ Ο ΘΕΟС ΙΛΛСΤΗΡΙΟΝ
ΔΙΛ ΤΗС ΠΙСΤΕШС ΕΝ ΤШ ΛΥΤΟΥ ΛΙΜΛΤΙ

THEY ARE JUSTIFIED AS A GIFT
THROUGH HIS GRACE
THROUGH THE *APOLUTROSIS*
THAT IS IN CHRIST JESUS
WHOM GOD SET FORTH AS THE *ILASTERION*
THROUGH FAITH IN HIS BLOOD

Romans 3:24–25

In this passage, two words have been left untranslated. *Apolutrosis* denotes the process by which a person was released or redeemed from captivity by the payment of a ransom (*lutron*).[10] I have no idea what contemporary people might imagine when they read the conventional translation of this word, "redemption." Perhaps redeeming discount coupons at a grocery store? It's a complicated concept; it doesn't answer to anything in our vocabulary. Let's leave it as *apolutrosis* and think, when we read it, of the process by which a person was released from captivity by the payment of a ransom.

Ilasterion is an even more alien concept to modern readers. The element *ilas* means "mercy" or "pity," and the larger word *ilasterion* was used to describe the covering of the biblical ark of the covenant, on which sacrificial blood was sprinkled. It was the "place of mercy," or in archaic English, the "mercy seat."[11] Paul was claiming that Christ became the *ilasterion* on behalf of human beings, an offering for sin.

What sights, smells, sounds, textures, and tastes would the word *ilasterion* have suggested to hearers in the ancient world? Ancient people made offerings to the gods in a huge variety of ways, but some common elements of these offerings were as follows.

10. Kittel and Friedrich, *Theological Dictionary of the New Testament*, 4:351–56 (ἀπολύτρωσις, s.v. "λύω"), esp. 320–23.

11. Kittel and Friedrich, *Theological Dictionary of the New Testament*, 3:318–23 (ἱλαστήριον, s.v. "ἵλεως").

- A person made **an offering to a god that represented the offering of herself or himself.** The offering had to be from the very best of their produce (for example, grain or oil) or of their flocks. The offering had to be "unblemished" (e.g., Exod 12:5). The sight of an offering brought to an altar, the sight of the altar itself prepared for the offerings, and the sight of a priest accepting the offering might have come into the mind of ancient people when they heard words associated with offerings. Those who were religiously sensitive would have thought of the sacrifice as representing the offering of themselves.

- The offering was **transformed by cooking it** as a loaf or cake in the case of grain offerings or as roasted meat in the case of animal offerings. The textures or feeling of these offerings or the textures of the altar and its accouterments might have come into the minds of ancient people when they heard words associated with offering and sacrifice. They might also have thought of the sounds made by a fire, the sounds of the priests attending the altar, and perhaps the words that the priest pronounced as the offering was cooked.

- **The smoke of the offering rose** and was understood as a sign of divine acceptance of the offering (Lev 1:9, 13), especially if the smoke rose straight up. The sight and smell of the smoke rising from the sacrifice would have come to the minds of ancient people familiar with these practices.

- **The worshiper** and perhaps the priests who had made the offering **consumed it in a sacred meal representing restored fellowship** between each other and the gods to whom the offering had been made. The taste of these offerings might have come into the minds of ancient people familiar with these practices.[12]

This last point is particularly important. Offerings almost always culminated in a meal in which the offering was eaten together as a sign of restored fellowship or friendship, so the meanings of feasting and an offering to the gods were closely related.

Early Christians knew by personal contact all of these meanings associated with offerings and sacrifices, and they understood Christ's life, death, and resurrection as fulfilling these elements of offerings.

---

12. Some of these aspects of ancient sacrifices are laid out in Gihr, *Holy Sacrifice of the Mass*, 26–31.

- **Christ's whole life was understood as his pure offering**: Christ "of-fered himself without blemish to God" (Heb 9:14). What Christ offered was "himself." It was not simply Christ's death that became the *ilasterion*, it was Christ himself.

- **Christ "died for our sins according to the scriptures"** (1 Corinthians 15:3): he "entered once for all into the Holy Place, not with the blood of goats and calves, but with his own blood" (Heb 9:12).

- **Christ's resurrection represented God's acceptance of his offering**, just as the fragrant and rising smoke of an offering represented divine acceptance of it: "live in love as Christ loved us and gave himself up for us, a fragrant offering and sacrifice to God" (Eph 5:2; also 2 Cor 2:16).

- **The Lord's Supper was understood as the fellowship meal that culminated Christ's offering**, where his body and blood were shared with his followers (1 Cor 11:23–26).[13]

The Lord's Supper had a central place in early Christian communities because the early Christians understood that all the elements of Christ's offering were completed when they participated in his offering by receiving the offering of his own body and blood.[14]

It's important to understand, further, that **the Supper was instituted in the context of a particular offering: the offering of the Passover lamb**, a sign of the deliverance of God's people from slavery in Egypt. The account of the Supper that Paul transmitted in 1 Corinthians 11 incorporates a number of elements of the Passover meal:

ΟΤΙ Ο ΚΥΡΙΟC ΙΗCΟΥC
ΕΝ ΤΗ ΝΥΚΤΙ Η ΠΑΡΕΔΙΔΕΤΟ
ΕΛΑΒΕΝ ΑΡΤΟΝ
ΚΑΙ ΕΥΧΑΡΙCΤΗCΑC ΕΚΛΑCΕΝ . . .
ωCΑΥΤωC ΚΑΙ ΤΟ ΠΟΤΗΡΙΟΝ
ΜΕΤΑ ΤΟ ΔΕΙΠΝΗCΑΙ

13. Nicholas Gihr demonstrated some of these aspects of Christ's sacrifice—though typical of Catholic dogmatic theology of his age, he separated the "bloody sacrifice" of Christ on the cross from the "perpetual sacrifice" of Christ in the Eucharist (Gihr, *Holy Sacrifice of the Mass*, 47–100).

14. Young, *Sacrifice and the Death of Christ*, 98–100, and esp. the last paragraph on 99.

THAT THE LORD JESUS
ON THE NIGHT IN WHICH HE WAS BETRAYED
TOOK BREAD
AND HAVING GIVEN THANKS HE BROKE IT . . .
LIKEWISE ALSO THE CUP AFTER EATING

1 Corinthians 11:23–25

This passage has direct parallels in the Gospels of Matthew (16:16–30), Mark (14:22–25), and Luke (22:14–20). The blessing of unleavened bread and the offering of cups of wine are recognizable parts of the Passover ritual.

The Passover meal combined three things together that would be transformed and incorporated into the Christian celebration of the Lord's Supper. The Passover meal had 1) **a sacred narrative**, the narrative of God's work in rescuing Israel from its bondage in Egypt; 2) an **offering commemorating this rescue** or deliverance, and this involved all the elements of ancient offerings described previously; and 3) **a shared meal** in which the offered lamb was consumed by participants.

The Christian Supper would involve three similar elements: 1) **the narrative of Christ's saving work** (the gospel), 2) **consuming the elements of bread and wine** as participating in Christ's offering, and 3) **the fellowship meal**, although as we have seen the actual meal came to be separated from the sacred ritual that commemorated Christ's offering even in the time of Saint Paul. Protestant churches continued to use the language of offerings in their doctrinal statements and liturgies.[15] Some of the evangelical Gospel songs of the late 1800s and early 1900s utilize lavish blood imagery derived from the ancient practice of offerings.

The Supper and the Presence of Christ

In the Passover meal, the body of the offered lamb was present on the table when Jesus said the following words:

15. For example, the Articles of Religion of the Church of England speak of Christ's work as "The one oblation of Christ finished upon the Cross" (the heading of Article 31 in Pelikan and Hotchkiss, *Creeds and Confessions*, 2:536). Similarly, the service for the Lord's Supper in the 1662 *Book of Common Prayer* states that Christ "made there (by his one oblation of himself once offered) a full, perfect, and sufficient sacrifice, oblation, and satisfaction for the sins of the whole world" (in Cummings, *Book of Common Prayer*, 402).

ΤΟΥΤΟ ΜΟΥ ЄСΤΙΝ ΤΟ СШΜΑ
ΤΟ ΥΠЄΡ ΥΜШΝ
ΤΟΥΤΟ ΠΟΙЄΙΤЄ
ЄΙС ΤΗΝ ЄΜΗΝ ΑΝΑΜΝΗСΙΝ. . .
ΤΟΥΤΟ ΤΟ ΠΟΤΗΡΙΟΝ
Η ΚΑΙΝΗ ΔΙΑΘΗΚΗ ЄСΤΙΝ
ЄΝ ΤШ ЄΜШ ΑΙΜΑΤΙ
ΤΟΥΤΟ ΠΟΙЄΙΤЄ ОСΑΚΙС ЄΑΝ ΠΙΝΗΤЄ
ЄΙС ΤΗΝ ЄΜΗΝ ΑΝΑΜΝΗСΙΝ

THIS IS MY BODY
THAT IS FOR YOU
DO THIS IN MY MEMORY . . .
THIS CUP
IS THE NEW COVENANT
IN MY BLOOD
DO THIS AS OFTEN AS YOU DRINK IT
IN MY MEMORY

1 Corinthians 11:24–25

Jesus identified his own body and blood with the bread he broke and the wine he blessed, suggesting that his own body and blood were offered as a parallel to the lamb offered and consumed in the Passover meal. His blood was a "new covenant" in contrast to the older celebration of Passover. Just as Jews remembered the narrative of their deliverance at Passover, so Jesus asked his disciples to eat the bread and drink the cup "in my memory." The understanding of Jesus' life as an offering to God originated with Jesus himself.

As a fellowship meal culminated ancient offerings, the Lord's Supper culminates the self-offering of Jesus Christ. It is the richest, deepest means of proclaiming the gospel, even though it takes some explanation to bring modern people into an understanding of it. Welcome to the depths of Christian belief. The holy feast is a sign of our fellowship or communion with each other and with Jesus Christ.

How do we understand this distinctive moment of communion with Christ? How do we understand "This [bread] is my body that is for you . . . The cup is the new covenant in my blood"? **Christians through the centuries have claimed to experience the presence of Jesus Christ in**

receiving the Lord's Supper.[16] Paul himself wrote of those who approach the Supper unworthily, "without discerning the body" ("the Lord's body" in some manuscripts; 1 Cor 11:29). Some Protestants have squirmed over this passage, rationalizing it by saying that "the body" must refer to the church, the gathered community, though in its place in 1 Corinthians, it follows very close after Jesus' own saying, "This [bread] is my body that is for you" (verse 24). The early Christian writer Saint Ignatius of Antioch, writing in the decade of the 110s AD, wrote of church members who "abstain from Eucharist [thanksgiving] and prayer because they refuse to acknowledge that the Eucharist is the flesh of our savior Jesus Christ, which suffered for our sins and which the Father by his goodness raised up."[17]

Medieval Catholic theologians developed a more sophisticated explanation of the manner of Christ's presence. Distinguishing between the substance of a thing and its outward appearances, Saint Thomas Aquinas and other medieval theologians maintained that **the substance of bread and wine are entirely replaced by the substance of Christ's body and blood, even though they retain the external appearance of bread and wine.** This teaching, traditionally called "**transubstantiation,**" became formal Catholic doctrine late in the Middle Ages, although in more recent Catholic doctrinal statements, such as the *Catechism of the Catholic Church* (1992), the theory seems to have taken second place to a more general claim of the human presence of Christ in the celebration of the Mass.[18] Consistent with this outlook, pious Catholics refuse to refer to the elements after their consecration as "bread" or "wine"; they are "the most sacred body" of Christ and "the most sacred blood."

Martin Luther and the Lutheran communities that followed him did not accept the philosophical underpinnings of this medieval view, the distinction between the substance of a thing and its outward appearances. In their view, the true human body and blood of Jesus Christ are present on earth in the Supper in addition to the elements of bread and wine. Luther

16. See the section on eucharist in World Council of Churches Faith and Order Commission, *Baptism, Eucharist and Ministry*, ¶¶ 6 and 14.

17. See Ignatius of Antioch's *Letter to the Smyrnaeans* 6:2 in the translation of Holmes, *Apostolic Fathers*, 254 (text) and 255 (translation).

18. Doctrinal Decree of the Fourth Lateran Council, item 3 (in Pelikan and Hotchkiss, *Creeds and Confessions*, 1:741–42); Council of Trent, "Decree Concerning the Most Holy Sacrament of the Eucharist," chapters 1 and 4 (in Pelikan and Hotchkiss, *Creeds and Confessions*, 2:843 and 845); *Catechism of the Catholic Church* ¶¶ 1356–81 (in Catholic Church, *Catechism of the Catholic Church*, 342–48).

insisted that "this is my body" meant exactly and literally that. **The doctrine of Lutheran churches has continued to insist that Christ's human body and blood are present in the celebration of the Supper.**[19]

Not all the Protestants went along with Luther's understanding of Christ's presence in the Supper. **John Calvin** could not accept the idea that the human body and blood of Christ were present on earth because, he pointed out, the body of Christ had ascended to heaven. Nevertheless, Calvin taught that there is **a unique spiritual power available to those who receive with faith**, a distinctive presence that is "as if" Jesus Christ were bodily present.[20]

Yet others associated with the Reformer **Ulrich Zwingli**, maintained that the presence of Christ in the Supper is **not a unique or distinctive presence, but is the same as "whenever two or three are gathered" in Christ's name** (Matt 18:20). Doctrinal statements of Reformed churches allow for either the Calvinist view or the Zwinglian view of the presence of Christ in the Supper.[21]

In contemporary ecumenical dialogues, debates about the mode of Christ's presence from the age of the reformations have been overshadowed by **the mutual rediscovery of other depths of meaning in the Lord's Supper**: the understanding of the Supper as the culmination of Christ's offering, the recognition that "memory" is a crucial element in the meaning of the Supper, the understanding of the Supper as a sign and foretaste of the coming reign of God (see chapter 7), and the celebration of the Supper as our present participation in the heavenly banquet in which saints on earth and in heaven share fellowship with Christ and with each other.[22]

---

19. Augsburg Confession 10 (in Pelikan and Hotchkiss, *Creeds and Confessions*, 2:64); Luther's *Small Catechism* 5 or 6 on "The Sacrament of the Altar" (in Pelikan and Hotchkiss, *Creeds and Confessions*, 2:43); Formula of Concord, Epitome 7 (in Pelikan and Hotchkiss, *Creeds and Confessions*, 2:185–90); see Schmid, *Doctrinal Theology*, 555–82.

20. Calvin, *Institutes* 4.17.10–12 (in Calvin, *Institutes of the Christian Religion*, 2:1370–73).

21. Westminster Confession 29 (in Pelikan and Hotchkiss, *Creeds and Confessions*, 2:642–44); Heidelberg Catechism, questions 75–79 (in Pelikan and Hotchkiss, *Creeds and Confessions*, 2:443–45); Anglican Articles of Religion 28–31 (in Pelikan and Hotchkiss, *Creeds and Confessions*, 2:535–36); Anglican Catechism (in Pelikan and Hotchkiss, *Creeds and Confessions*, 2:370); Basis of Union of The United Church of Canada, Article 16, para. 3 (in Pelikan and Hotchkiss, *Creeds and Confessions*, 3:450); see Heppe, *Reformed Dogmatics*, 627–56.

22. See the section on Eucharist in World Council of Churches Faith and Order Commission, *Baptism, Eucharist and Ministry*, ¶¶ 2–26.

The Form of the Lord's Supper

How did early Christians celebrate the Supper? For one thing, early Christian literature indicates that the synagogue practice of reading or reciting and commenting on the Scriptures had become a part of the Christian celebration. The recitation of portions of the Torah was itself part of the Passover meal, so these elements came together naturally.

The early Christian writer Saint Justin Martyr, writing around the 140s AD, described the practice of the Roman congregation in that era. He indicated that Christians came together on Sunday mornings, and their worship followed this sequence:

- Christian as well as Jewish **Scriptures** ("the memoirs of the apostles or the writings of the prophets") were read.

- The presider offered a **message** to participants based on the Scriptures.

- The congregation offered **prayers**, standing.

- **Bread, wine, and water** were presented.

- The presider offered **prayers of thanksgiving**.

- The people responded by saying, **"Amen"**.

- The elements of bread and wine were **distributed**.[23]

The first three items seem to reflect the synagogue practice of reading or reciting Scriptures, offering instruction and exhortation as commentary on the Scriptures, and then prayer. Earlier scholars of liturgical history presupposed that this also involved the chanting of Psalms, presuming that Psalm chanting was part of the synagogue practice. More recent historical research has shown no evidence for Psalm singing or chanting in either the synagogue services or the early Christian services at this time, although the Psalms might have been read or recited along with other Scriptures.[24] In some cases, congregations had copies of Jewish Scriptures ("the writings of the prophets"), typically in Greek translation, and various Christian writings ("the memoirs of the apostles"), though at this point there was no standard collection of Christian Scriptures. In many cases, congregations had few or no written texts of the Scriptures, and in that case they had

23. See Justin Martyr, *1 Apol.* 67:1–5 (in Justin Martyr, *Justin, Philosopher and Martyr: Apologies*, 258 and 260 (text), 259 and 261 (translation).

24. See essay 8, "On the Question of Psalmody in the Ancient Synagogue," in McKinnon, *Temple, the Church Fathers*, 95–96.

to recite portions of the Scriptures from memory, following the protocols for oral transmission (reciting and hearing in the presence of witnesses) discussed above.

The remaining items have to do with the celebration of the Supper itself. Bread and wine were presented, and the presider offered "prayers and thanksgivings." Here the word for "thanksgivings" in the language of the early Christian communities is the root of our word "Eucharist," and it invokes Jesus' actions in giving thanks in the institution of the Supper (1 Cor 11:24; Luke 17:19). The prayer offered by the presider would evolve into the great prayer of thanksgiving, the central prayer in the celebration of the Supper. The people indicated their consent by saying "Amen," then the elements over which thanks had been offered were distributed to the worshipers and also brought to those who were unable to attend.

As simple as it is, **the pattern of worship indicated in this passage from the second Christian century has remained the basic shape or structure for celebrating the Lord's Supper.**[25] Some early sources indicate that candidates for baptism (catechumens) were dismissed before the presentation of bread and wine, so they were permitted to hear the reading of the Scriptures and the interpretation of the Scriptures and to be present for the congregation's prayers, but they were not allowed to stay for the celebration of the Supper. The dismissal of the catechumens marked a break in the service between the first part, involving Scripture recitation or reading, preaching, and prayer, and the later part of the service, which involved the celebration of the Supper.

Alas, at this point there were no church buildings, no pews, no pew cushions, no organs or pianos or electric guitars, no sitting still for organ preludes or postludes, no hymnals or prayer books or monthly missalettes, no sign-in sheets with the "I want to talk to a pastor" check box, no sound systems, no electric lights, and no "exit" signs. There were no Bibles except for very rare and precious copies of biblical books or writings, and only a few literate members of the congregation could read these. We are not even sure of the extent to which music was a regular part of these services, although there are a few references to Christian music in the New Testament and other early Christian literature.[26]

25. See the section on Eucharist in World Council of Churches Faith and Order Commission, *Baptism, Eucharist and Ministry,* ¶¶ 27–33.

26. See the passages from the New Testament and from second-century Christian literature given in McKinnon, *Music in Early Christian Literature,* 12–27.

The fourth century AD witnessed a number of developments in the Christian celebration of the Lord's Supper. For one thing, the toleration of Christianity granted by the emperors Constantine and Licinius from AD 318 enabled Christians to build public spaces for worship. The chanting of Psalms became customary from the later 300s, in addition to the reading of Old Testament and New Testament Scriptures (see the next chapter).[27] Christian congregations grew as a result of toleration, and bishops deputized Christian elders (also called "presbyters" or "priests") to preside at the Lord's Supper.

Common Practices

A few years ago, I attended a Church of Christ congregation in Dallas. One of the most radical Protestant groups in the United States, the Churches of Christ refuse to accept any doctrinal basis except the New Testament itself, and do not acknowledge Christian traditions beyond the New Testament period. But, consistent with the New Testament, the Churches of Christ observe the Lord's Supper every Sunday, and the service I attended had all the marks of historic Christian celebration.

The congregation "met on the first day of the week to break bread" (Acts 20:7). After some initial singing and prayers, the New Testament was read aloud, and the pastor preached a sermon based on the Gospel passage that had been read. Later in the service, an elder of the congregation offered a simple prayer of thanksgiving for the bread and a prayer of thanksgiving for the wine, then the elements were distributed to the congregation. The congregation's singing involved some simple hymns and some more elaborate musical pieces, though in the style of the Churches of Christ, all the music was sung without instrumental accompaniment.[28]

It occurred to me how similar this service was to the celebration of the Lord's Supper described by Justin Martyr in Rome in the second Christian century. All the elements Justin described appeared in the Church of Christ service, in just about the order Justin described. This might not be a complete coincidence: the Churches of Christ have produced some excellent scholars of early Christianity, including scholars who have studied Justin

27. Augustine, *Conf.* 9:7; my translation based on the Latin text given in Augustine, *Les Confessions*, 14:98.

28. I describe here the service at Preston Road Church of Christ in Dallas, Texas, on Sunday, March 6, 2011.

and the second-century church.[29] But it more likely reflects what is simply a common and almost natural Christian pattern for celebrating the Supper. I would have found the same elements had I attended a nearby Catholic or Orthodox or Anglican service.

This is not to make light of enormous differences in Christian worship cultures. But it is to claim that, across the differences of languages, cultures, and musical styles, and across the centuries from the time of Jesus to the present, there remains a core of worship practices common to Christian communities. **The holy feast, "the breaking of bread," is at the center of these common practices.** It is the richest unfolding of the depth of the gospel, the proclamation through words and bread and wine of the self-giving work of God in Christ that Christians continue to proclaim until his coming again.

29. I refer here to the work of Dr. Everett Ferguson of Abilene Christian University.

CHAPTER 5

A Life of Self-Giving Love

I WANT TO INVITE you to a deeper Christian faith. The last chapter explored the Lord's Supper as it reveals the depth of God's self-offering in Jesus Christ. But if God has given God's own self for us in the human person of Jesus Christ, what does God expect in return from us? According to the old book called *Devarim* or Deuteronomy, here's what God expects from us:

ואהבת את יהוה אלהיך
בכל־לבבך ובכל־נפשך ובכל־מאדך

AND YOU SHALL LOVE יהוה YOUR GOD
WITH ALL YOUR HEART
AND WITH ALL YOUR SOUL
AND WITH ALL YOUR MIGHT

Deuteronomy 6:5

When asked which commandment was the greatest, Jesus repeated this passage from *Devarim* with just a slight difference:

ΚΑΙ ΑΓΑΠΗϹΕΙϹ ΚΥΡΙΟΝ ΤΟΝ ΘΕΟΝ ϹΟΥ
ΕΞ ΟΛΗϹ ΤΗϹ ΚΑΡΔΙΑϹ ϹΟΥ
ΚΑΙ ΕΞ ΟΛΗϹ ΤΗϹ ΨΥΧΗϹ ϹΟΥ
ΚΑΙ ΕΞ ΟΛΗϹ ΤΗϹ ΔΙΑΝΟΙΑϹ ϹΟΥ
ΚΑΙ ΕΞ ΟΛΗϹ ΤΗϹ ΙϹΧΥΟϹ ϹΟΥ

AND YOU SHALL LOVE THE LORD YOUR GOD
WITH ALL YOUR HEART
AND WITH ALL YOUR SOUL
AND WITH ALL YOUR UNDERSTANDING
AND WITH ALL YOUR STRENGTH

Mark 12:30

In addition to "heart," "soul," and "strength," Jesus added "understanding" or "mind." It's probably not a significant change because the Hebrew word for "heart" includes the "mind" or "understanding" in addition to what we would think of as the "heart" as the center of affections.

But the point here is not at all to divide up a human being into "heart," "soul," "strength," and "understanding." A consistent feature of Hebrew literature is to use a sequence of things like this to mean, basically, the whole of a thing. In this case, these elements add up to the whole of a human being. **We are to love God with everything we have and everything we are. In response to God's self-offering in Jesus Christ, we offer ourselves back to God.**

If this sounds like a harsh demand that we "surrender all" to God and trash ourselves in the process, think of these words as the words of a lover to her beloved. When you're in love, you want the one you love, you passionately desire everything about them. You want it all: heart, soul, understanding, and strength. Think of the great commandment as the words of a lover to her beloved. God is the lover and you are the object of God's passionate desire. **What God wants from you is what a lover always wants. God wants all of you.**

Giving our lives back to God involves some things we do on our own, like individual prayer and devotional Bible study. We'll take up those practices in the next chapter. But **giving our lives to God also involves some things we do as participants in Christian communities**, like the blessing of marriages and Christian vocations. **This chapter will focus on ways in which Christian communities "hallow" or consecrate the lives of Christians.** Chapter 3 has already considered baptism, confirmation, and the anointing associated with baptism in many churches. Chapter 4 has considered the Lord's Supper. This chapter considers Christian practices associated with the hallowing of life beyond initiation and the Lord's Supper, practices associated with repentance and the pronouncement of forgiveness, marriage, ordination and other ways of recognizing Christian vocations, healing, Christian burial and memorial practices, and other occasional ways of hallowing the life of an individual or a community.

The Life 1: Baptism and Christian Initiation

Chapter 3 has discussed the holy bath of baptism as the gateway to the Christian life. It is one element in a process of Christian initiation that also involves conversion (repentance for sin and turning to Christ), training in the faith, and profession of the faith. In many Christian communities the process of Christian initiation also involves anointing and one's first communion in a Christian community. Everything that follows in this chapter builds on what had already happened in baptism and Christian initiation; **baptism is the seed of a new life from which a holy life in Christ grows.**

The Life 2: Repentance, Confession, and the Pronouncement of Forgiveness

If you haven't figured this out yet, I regret to inform you that Christians sometimes screw up after baptism. Early Christian communities maintained very high standards for their communities and considered a number of sins—such as falling away from the faith during a time of persecution—not only as offenses against God, but also as offenses against the community of believers. They considered persons known to have committed obvious sins against the community as having excluded themselves from the community by their actions. The letter to the Hebrews suggests that for some offenses, it was not possible to be reconciled (Heb 6:4–6). Some Christian converts actually postponed their baptism to the time of their death so that they could avoid sin after baptism!

It is likely that postponing baptism until the moment before death does actually reduce the chances of sinning after baptism, but Christians eventually figured out that God can see around this ruse. The second-century document called *The Shepherd of Hermas* offered a one-time-only offer of forgiveness for sins after baptism.[1] After Christianity came to be tolerated in the fourth century, the issue of how to deal with professed Christians who separated themselves by committing outward sins (like those who had

---

1. See *Shepherd of Hermas* in Holmes, *Apostolic Fathers*, 454–685. The offer of a one-time forgiveness of sin after baptism is repeated many times through the work, beginning at vision 1, verse 9 (Holmes, *Apostolic Fathers*, 456–57).

renounced Christ or their Christian faith during the times of persecution) became even more critical.

But we have to pay attention to two matters about this. First, **the sins they were concerned with were not personal sins**, sins between you and God. They were concerned with outward or obvious sins, like stealing, or worshiping other gods, **sins that were outward and visible offenses against the Christian community**.

Second, **the exclusion of a person from the community did not mean that God couldn't forgive them**. Again, that's God's business. In the eyes of Christian communities, it didn't even mean that the community itself was doing the excluding. As they saw it, a person who violated the vow he took at baptism had already excluded himself from the fellowship of the church. The community's work was to say, "Well, yes, he excluded himself from us by his action." The Christian community was concerned with offenses against the community and eventually with reconciling to the community those who had offended it.

The letter of James in the New Testament encourages Christians to confess their sins to each other and to pray for each other:

ⲉⲝⲟⲙⲟⲗⲟⲅⲉⲓⲥⲑⲉ ⲟⲩⲛ ⲁⲗⲗⲏⲗⲟⲓⲥ ⲦⲀⲤ ⲀⲘⲀⲣⲦⲓⲀⲤ
ⲕⲁⲓ ⲉⲩⲭⲉⲥⲑⲉ ⲩⲡⲉⲣ ⲁⲗⲗⲏⲗⲱⲛ ⲟⲡⲱⲥ ⲓⲁⲑⲏⲦⲉ

CONFESS THEN TO ONE ANOTHER YOUR SINS
AND PRAY FOR EACH OTHER
THAT YOU MAY BE HEALED

James 5:16

The expression "that you may be healed" probably refers to the "healing" of sin, envisioned as a disease that can "infect" us. Christians were to confess their sins to each other, and the words of Jesus at the conclusion of John's Gospel (John 20:22–23) maintain that if Christians forgive the sins of any, they are forgiven.

Christians have practiced the pronouncement of forgiveness, following this biblical mandate, but **does this mean that Christians should pronounce that everyone's sins are forgiven automatically?** A general consensus through Christian history has been that **we can pronounce forgiveness** following the mandate of John 20:22–23 **when we are convinced that a person is sincere in their repentance**. But this raises the question of

how we can know if a person has sincerely repented of her sins. Would crying, for example, convince you that a person is sincere in her repentance?
Crying was one of the criteria by which early Christian communities tried
to discern if a person was truly penitent.

The practice of hearing a fellow Christian's confession of sin, discerning their sincerity in repentance, and pronouncing forgiveness has been
enacted in a variety of ways, some more and some less formal. In Catholic
tradition, this practice evolved into the formal sacrament of penance and
reconciliation in which an ordained priest serves as the minister of the sacrament. As a test of sincerity, the priest may ask a Christian who repents
of his sin for a sign of repentance, called a "penance." He might ask, for
example, if a person was willing to return something they had stolen. Or he
might ask if they would say repeated prayers in a case where reparation for
their sin could not be made directly.[2]

In the time of the reformations, Protestants perceived that a penance
was a good work done in exchange for forgiveness, and they objected to
the Catholic practice of penance as a form of works-righteousness. But that
wasn't how the Catholic Church understood a penance. In the Catholic sacrament, forgiveness is not contingent on the believer's performing the act of
penance; it is the believer's sincerity in promising to perform the penance
that convinces the priest that he can pronounce forgiveness on behalf of
Christ and the church.

The Reformer Martin Luther continued the practice of hearing confessions and pronouncing absolution. The Augsburg Confession of 1530
lists confession and penance following baptism and the Lord's Supper, as if
it were a third sacrament along with them.[3] Luther's treatise on *The Babylonian Captivity of the Church* named penance as a sacrament at one point,
but as the treatise progressed, Luther clarified that penance involves a restoration of the grace given in baptism.[4] Luther did believe that any Christian—not necessarily an ordained minister—could hear the confession of

---

2. Catholic Church, *Catechism of the Catholic Church*, ¶ 1460 (in American translation, 367).

3. Augsburg Confession, in the section on common teachings, items 11 and 12,
following baptism (item 9) and the Lord's Supper (item 10); in Pelikan and Hotchkiss,
Creeds and Confessions, 2:64.

4. Luther's discussion of the sacramental status of penance is in his treatise on *The
Babylonian Captivity of the Church*, the section identified as "the Sacrament of Penance";
in Luther, *Three Treatises*, 206–18.

another Christian and pronounce absolution if she was convinced that a person had truly repented.

In other Protestant communities, the confession of sin and the pronouncement of forgiveness are likely to be much more informally handled—for example, in a private meeting with the pastor of a congregation. Many Protestant communities state formally that "confessional confidences" are to be held in strictest confidence and that the violation of such confidential information can be grounds for removal of clergy from the ministry.[5]

However formally or informally it may be done, **most Christian communities practice some form of confession and the pronouncement of forgiveness**. It's one of the ways in which communities hallow the lives of their participants and hold them accountable to the promises they make at baptism and at their profession of Christian faith.

The Life 3: The Lord's Supper
(Holy Communion, Eucharist, Mass, Qurbana)

The holy feast discussed in chapter 4 forms Christians for the holy life by its regular reading of the Scriptures; its proclamation of the gospel in preaching and in the words of the liturgy itself; and its repeated and character-forming messages of reconciliation and atonement, a fellowship meal, and the promise of Christ's presence. **In liturgically structured worship traditions, the Supper also contains a communal confession of sin and absolution**. This differs from the private confession envisioned in the previous section, but offers yet another opportunity for Christians to say, in solidarity with a community, that they have fallen short of God's call, they repent (turn around), and they receive the word of Christ's forgiveness that empowers them to move forward again in the way of self-giving love.

The Life 4: Blessing the Single Life

Jesus set the example of an unmarried life dedicated to God. When his followers suggested that "It is better not to marry," Jesus did not deny this, but replied, "Not everyone can accept this teaching, but only those to whom it is given" (Matt 19:10–11). Similarly, Saint Paul wrote in the first letter to the Corinthians,

5. For example, in *Book of Discipline*, ¶ 341.5.

ⲗⲉⲅⲱ ⲇⲉ ⲧⲟⲓⲥ ⲁⲅⲁⲙⲟⲓⲥ ⲕⲁⲓ ⲧⲁⲓⲥ ⲭⲏⲣⲁⲓⲥ
ⲕⲁⲗⲟⲛ ⲁⲩⲧⲟⲓⲥ ⲉⲁⲛ ⲙⲉⲓⲛⲱⲥⲓⲛ ⲱⲥ ⲕⲁⲅⲱ

BUT I SAY TO THE UNMARRIED AND WIDOWS
IT IS WELL FOR THEM TO REMAIN AS I ALSO AM

1 Corinthians 7:8

Some modern translations, such as the NRSV, say "it is well for them to remain *unmarried* as I am." The word "unmarried" is not actually in the text at that point, but the meaning is there, because Paul added immediately after this: "But if they do not practice self control, let them marry, for it is better to marry than to burn" (7:9). Beyond Jesus and Paul, there were plenty of examples of unmarried Christians in the early centuries, and Christian communities encouraged believers to remain unmarried.

In the early 300s AD, just about the time when Christianity was tolerated in the Roman Empire, **many Christians in Egypt chose to live a single life in the desert devoted to fasting and prayer**. They thought of themselves as following Jesus literally, and their lives of self-denial stood in contrast to the easier form of Christianity that toleration had made possible. They were called "monks," which in the Greek language means "lone" or "single" people. Do not imagine these monks to be like the sisters in *The Sound of Music*. These folks probably looked more like Hindu holy men or perhaps like hippies camped out in the desert by themselves. No rules. Go to the desert. Fast. Pray. Fight the demons.

Some of the early monks led seriously undisciplined lives, and it was not just that boring churchy people had a problem with that. Some superstar monks could live by themselves for long periods in the desert, but others found that they needed communities for support and began organizing **communes of Christian monks**. Colonies of monks began spreading through the Mediterranean world. As Western Roman society began to disintegrate in the 400s AD, monastic communities provided havens of shelter and stability.

In the early 500s AD, the Italian monk **Benedict of Nursia** established a series of communities under a rule he devised. Benedict's *Rule* became the classic pattern for Western monasteries. The *Rule* insisted that a person who wanted to enter the monastic life needed to be tested for a period of years to be sure that he or she could make a permanent commitment to the single life devoted to service to God and to other people. Once tested, the candidate made a lifelong commitment to the monastic life. Benedictine monasteries became not only havens of social stability, but centers of learning and places where Christians could extend charity and hospitality to others.[6]

With the pattern of a permanent, lifelong commitment to monastic life, **both Eastern and Western Christian communities blessed the commitments of women and men who chose the monastic life.** Latin-speaking Western churches eventually decided that everyone who was ordained as a priest, whether members of a monastic order or not, should be committed to the single life. In the Western church in the Middle Ages, a Christian had two basic choices in life: to be married, or to be single as a member of a monastic community or clergy. Eastern Christian churches decided that married men could be priests, although they reserved the office of bishop for men who had been trained in monastic communities and thus single. In either case, Christian communities blessed these decisions for lifelong commitments to a single life.

Protestant churches have seldom made provisions for blessing the single life. At the time of the reformations they almost uniformly rejected the notion that clergy had to be single, and they did not establish monastic communities. Anglicans and some Protestant communities would later develop monastic communities, and there were other Protestant groups who had almost *de facto* instances of the single life committed to God. Early Methodist itinerant preachers in North America, for example, tended to be single men whose work practically ruled out the possibility of settling down and having families. Protestant communities also supported groups of single women committed to mission and ministry; some of these were self-identified in the 1800s as deaconesses. Scots Presbyterian minister George MacLeod rebuilt the ancient Christian abbey of Iona in 1938 and opened it as an ecumenical religious community. Ten years later, the Swiss Protestant Roger Schütz-Marsauche established an ecumenical religious community at Taizé in France that has attracted thousands of pilgrims.

The Life 5: Blessing Marriage

Marriages are one of the few occasions when non-churchgoing people are likely to show up in a Christian church. There's a natural tendency to think

6. See "The Rule of St. Benedict," chapter 58, in Benedict of Nursia, *Rule of Saint Benedict*, 186–91.

that marriage had a distinctly Christian meaning from ancient times, but that's not really the case. Saint Paul the apostle expressed this truly luke-warm view of marriage:

εl ΔE ΟΥΚ ΕΓΚΡΑΤΕΥΟΝΤΑΙ
ΓΑΜΗCΑΤΩCΑΝ
ΚΡΕΙΤΤΟΝ ΓΑΡ ΕCΤΙΝ ΓΑΜΗCΑΙ
Η ΠΥΡΟΥCΘΑΙ

BUT IF THEY DO NOT PRACTICE SEXUAL RESTRAINT
LET THEM MARRY
FOR IT IS BETTER TO MARRY
THAN TO BURN

1 Corinthians 7:9

Contemporary translations render "burn" as "burn with passion," per-haps to stave off the idea that "burn" could denote roasting in hell. Better to leave it ambiguous, in my view, as it appears to be in the original text. Either way, this passage really does not say much for marriage as the Chris-tian norm. As we have seen, Paul explicitly advocated the single life for Christians. His justification for marriage was a pastoral one. He recognized that in some cases the single life was not practical, and in such a case, it's "better" for people "to marry than to burn."

Early Christian communities did acknowledge marriages per-formed by civil authorities, and sometimes offered a blessing of a marriage. When Christians did come around to blessing marriages more formally, they cited Jesus' words about the divine institution of marriage (Matt 19:4–6; Mark 10:6–9) and the story in John's Gospel of Jesus provid-ing wine for the marriage feast at Cana of Galilee (John 2:1–11). This was a way of suggesting that Jesus himself had "blessed" the marriage. And he did, in the basic sense in which "to bless" means "to make happy." But there seem to have been no distinctly Christian rituals for marriage until well into the Middle Ages. Christian communities relied on civil ceremonies and then "blessed" or acknowledge the civil marriage. The rituals that came to be used for celebrating a Christian marriage were very similar to rituals used in medieval society to forge bonds between families by pronouncing oaths to each other.

A controversial work by John Boswell entitled *Same-Sex Unions in Premodern Europe* (1994) argued that, among the many forms of blessing of bonds between individuals and families in the Middle Ages, some were bonds uniting men together, thus what he called "same-sex unions" blessed by churches.[7] Critics were quick to point out that the "unions" to which Boswell referred were not explicitly sexual unions; most in fact were practical alliances for military or domestic support. But Boswell's research made us aware of the problematic fact that medieval Christian marriage ceremonies were grounded in common forms of contracts between families, contracts in which a woman could be exchanged in the same way as goods were exchanged.

Christian communities have historically insisted that a marriage commitment must be made for life. They require a pledge of faithfulness "till death do us part."[8] Jesus' words about the indissolubility of marriage (Matt 5:31–32; Mark 10:10–12; Luke 16:18) have made Christian communities **very reluctant to acknowledge divorces and to bless remarriage after divorce**. Christian communities have approached the possibility of remarriage after divorce in a variety of ways. The Catholic Church does not bless remarriages after divorce per se, but will bless a remarriage when an earlier marriage has been "nullified," that is, declared not to have been a valid Christian marriage. Nullification has been granted more liberally since the 1960s in response to pastoral concerns (like, "better to nullify than to burn"), though one could see liberal nullifications as a disguised way of blessing remarriage after what appears to be a divorce and often is, in fact, a civil divorce. Eastern Orthodox churches require a period of mourning after the dissolution of a marriage, a period in which formerly married persons grieve the "death" of their marriage. After such a period of mourning, a remarriage can be blessed by Orthodox churches. Conservative Protestant communities have historically refused to bless any remarriage after divorce, although other Protestant communities have come to bless remarriages, citing pastoral grounds ("better to remarry than to burn") for doing so.

In recent decades, the issue of **whether churches should bless same-sex marriages or unions** has also troubled traditional Christian communities. Saint Paul's words in Romans 1:26–27 (and surrounding verses)

---

7. Boswell, *Same-Sex Unions*.

8. The words of the marriage vows in the traditional service of the 1662 *Book of Common Prayer* in Cummings, *Book of Common Prayer*, 436.

condemn homoerotic acts in much the same way that Jesus' words cited above condemn remarriage after divorce.[9] How could Christian communities bless either remarriages after divorce, or same-sex unions, given the teachings of the Scriptures?

A minority of Christian communities in the last two decades have allowed the blessing of same-sex unions, increasingly described as marriages, citing similar pastoral considerations as led churches to acknowledge remarriages after divorce. The logic would be something like "better to bless a gay union than to burn." However, many churches that have found it relatively easy to allow remarriage after divorce have not allowed unions of gay or lesbian persons, despite the parallel issues raised in biblical texts, and the question of whether churches should bless such unions has been a divisive issue in recent decades, especially in older Protestant denominations.

The Life 6: Christian Vocations including Ordination and Consecration

The blessing of a marriage or a commitment to a single life is one way in which Christian communities hallow or sanctify the lives of Christians. Another way is in **blessing permanent decisions about one's calling or vocation as a Christian**. The Second Vatican Council declared, "For by the regeneration and anointing of the Holy Spirit the baptized are consecrated as a spiritual dwelling and a holy priesthood."[10] This means that all Christians share in Christ's work of ministry, and the ecumenical movement has emphasized the varied gifts that Christians have for ministry in the church beyond the ranks of ordained clergy.[11] In its own way, the Charismatic movement prominent from the 1970s emphasized the "spiritual gifts" (*cha-*

---

9. Although John Boswell argued that Romans 1:26–27 does not condemn homosexual acts or relationships (Boswell, *Christianity, Social Toleration, and Homosexuality*, 107–13), I find the arguments of Victor Paul Furnish and Richard B. Hays more historically credible. Furnish argues that Paul did condemn homoerotic acts, although Furnish makes the point that Paul did not have any sense of "homosexuality" in the modern sense (see Furnish, *Moral Teaching of Paul*, 84–88). Hays has made a case for a sense in which Paul did in fact condemn homosexual relationships per se (see Hays, *Moral Vision*, 383–89).

10. See Second Vatican Council, dogmatic constitution *Lumen Gentium* 2:10; in Pelikan and Hotchkiss, *Creeds and Confessions*, 3:581.

11. See section on ministry in World Council of Churches Faith and Order Commission, *Baptism, Eucharist and Ministry*, ¶¶ 1–6 and 32–33.

rismata; 1 Cor 12, 14) given by the Holy Spirit to Christians. All of God's people have ministries. One of the tasks of the Christian community is to recognize and celebrate those gifts and to bless or consecrate Christians as they seek to minister with the gifts they have received.

Since New Testament times, **Christian communities have set aside some persons for particular forms of ministry**. Sometimes this simply meant offering prayers for persons when they were about to embark on a particular mission or task. Here's how the Acts of the Apostles describes the blessing of Saul and Barnabas as they were sent off on a missionary journey:

ΤΟΤΕ ΝΗΣΤΕΥCΑΝΤΕC ΚΑΙ ΠΡΟCΕΥΖΑΜΕΝΟΙ
ΚΑΙ ΕΠΙΘΕΝΤΕC ΤΑC ΧΕΙΡΑC ΑΥΤΟΙC ΑΠΕΛΥCΑΝ

THEN AFTER FASTING AND PRAYING
THEY LAID HANDS ON THEM AND SENT THEM AWAY

Acts 13:3

The blessing involved the elements of fasting, prayer, the laying-on of hands, and then the sending away.

This blessing was for a particular mission, but the Scriptures record other blessings for permanent service. Acts 6:6 describes the blessing of a group of seven men who were set apart by the apostles with prayer and the laying-on of hands "to serve" in the distribution of food. The apostles did this in response to the complaints of "Hellenists," who said that their widows had been neglected. All seven men all seem to have Hellenistic names. (Basic principle of church administration: someone complains about something, and they get to be in charge of it.) The ministry of service for which these men were set apart became the office of "**deacon**," a title derived from the verb "to serve" or "minister" (Rom 16:1; 1 Tim 3:8–13) in the early Christian church.[12] Other early Christians were set apart for the offices of "**widow**" (1 Tim 5:9–16), "**elder**" (**or "presbyter" or "priest"**; 1 Tim 5:17–22; Titus 1:5–9; Rev 4:4),[13] and "**overseer**" (**or "bishop" or**

---

12. Kittel and Friedrich, *Theological Dictionary of the New Testament*, 2:88–93 (διάκονος, s.v. "διακονέω").

13. Kittel and Friedrich, *Theological Dictionary of the New Testament*, 6:651–80 (πρεσβύτερος, s.v. "πρέσβυς"), esp. 662–72.

"superintendent"; 1 Tim 3:1–7; Titus 1:5–9), though it's possible that "elder" and "overseer" originally designated the same office.[14]

By the 100s AD, a **pattern** had emerged in most Christian communities according to which there was **a single overseer or bishop** in each community who worked together with **a group of elders** and **a group of deacons**. The overseers or bishops represented the unity of the church in the region around the city, and councils of bishops from different cities and regions sometimes met to make critical decisions on behalf of wider Christian communities. **Bishops presided at the Lord's Supper, though by the 300s AD they had deputized elders (presbyters, priests) to serve in that role.** This pattern of the ministry of bishops (overseers, superintendents), elders (presbyters, priests), and deacons has remained fairly consistent in Christian communities since the early centuries.[15]

Christian communities celebrated the vocations of deacons and elders by **ordaining** them, and they recognized the vocation of bishops by ordaining or consecrating them to this office. Services for ordination and consecration involved the elements mentioned in the passage from the Acts of the Apostles given above: **fasting, prayer, and the laying-on of hands**. The custom grew that, when a bishop was consecrated, at least three other bishops should lay their hands on him. The laying-on of hands was seen as one of the signs of the continuity of the Christian community from the time of the apostles.

Did early Christians ordain women? The question may rely on the meaning of "ordain," not a term consistently used in the New Testament. Women were set aside for specific offices, such as the "widows" who were "enrolled" in their office according to 1 Timothy 5:9–16. **Women were designated as apostles**: "Greet Andronicus and Junia," Saint Paul wrote to the Romans, "my relatives who were in prison with me; they are prominent among the apostles, and they were in Christ before I was" (Rom 16:7). In the same chapter, he commended "Phoebe, a deacon of the church at Cenchreae," and he says of Phoebe that, "she has been a benefactor of many and of myself as well" (Rom 16:1–2). The word translated "benefactor" here can also be translated "assistant," and some have suggested that it could even

---

14. Kittel and Friedrich, *Theological Dictionary of the New Testament*, 2:615–20 (ἐπίσκοπος, s.v. "ἐπισκέπτομαι").

15. See section on ministry in World Council of Churches Faith and Order Commission, *Baptism, Eucharist and Ministry*, ¶¶ 19–25 and 28–31.

denote a person who is "set over others," and in this sense a rough equivalent of the word translated "bishop" that means "overseer."[16]

Despite these indications of women's leadership roles in early Christian churches, historic Christian communities have been very reluctant to ordain women as priests (presbyters/elders) or bishops. Some Eastern Orthodox churches, such as the Church of Greece, ordain women as deaconesses.[17] The Catholic Church is in full communion with at least one church—the Syriac Maronite Church of Antioch—that historically ordained women as deaconesses.[18] Despite this, the practice has not continued in churches in communion with the Catholic Church.

In the late 1800s and the early 1900s, **Holiness and Pentecostal churches** in the United States took the lead in ordaining women. Since the 1970s, **progressive Protestant groups** have also ordained women, though the process is ongoing and the goal of inclusion of women in the highest positions of leadership (e.g., as bishops or as pastors of very large churches) remains largely unfulfilled.[19]

The Life 7: Prayers for Healing and for the Dying

Christian communities bless and pray for persons facing serious illnesses or other challenges. The letter of James in the New Testament refers to this practice:

$$\text{ΛϹΘΕΝΕΙ ΤΙϹ ΕΝ ΥΜΙΝ}$$
$$\text{ΠΡΟϹΚΛΛΕϹΛϹΘω ΤΟΥϹ ΠΡΕϹΒΥΤΕΡΟΥϹ ΤΗϹ}$$
$$\text{ΕΚΚΛΗϹΙΛϹ}$$
$$\text{ΚΛΙ ΠΡΟϹΕΥΞΛϹΘωϹΛΝ ΕΠ ΛΥΤΟΝ}$$

---

16. See Fiorenza, "Missionaries, Apostles, Coworkers," 423–27. The quoted meaning, "set over others," is from the older lexicon of Thayer, *Thayer's Greek-English Lexicon*, 549, s.v. "προστάτις."

17. Ware, *Orthodox Church*, 292–93.

18. Pope Benedict XIV approved a set of canons referring explicitly to the ordination of deaconesses in the Maronite Church in 1741. They are given in Morin, *De Sacris Ecclesiae Ordinationibus*, 124–26. On the papal approval of these canons, see Dib, *History of the Maronite Church*, 130–38. On the broader historical issues of women's ordination in the Catholic Church, see Zagano, *Holy Saturday*, 76–110.

19. See section on ministry in World Council of Churches Faith and Order Commission, *Baptism, Eucharist and Ministry*, ¶ 18.

ΑΛΕΙΨΑΝΤΕϹ ΑΥΤΟΝ ΕΛΛΙѠ
ΕΝ ΤѠ ΟΝΟΜΑΤΙ ΤΟΥ ΚΗΡΙΟΥ

IS ANYONE SICK AMONG YOU
LET HIM CALL THE ELDERS OF THE CHURCH
LET THEM PRAY OVER HIM
ANOINTING HIM WITH OIL
IN THE NAME OF THE LORD

James 5:14

The elders (also translated "presbyters" or "priests") represent the community in offering prayers over the one they're concerned about. Anointing with oil was a common ancient practice. In this verse, the word for "anointing" is a different word than the more religious term denoting the anointing of Christ or the anointing of prophets, priests, and kings.[20] The word used here describes the simple use of olive oil as an ointment, an expression of comfort and care.

In the Western church in the Middle Ages, the ritual of anointing the sick came to be associated with **prayers for the dying**. With this understanding of the anointing, it became the custom to perform the rite only when a person was believed to be near death. For a long period in Catholic history it was called **"the last anointing" (extreme unction)** or **"last rites."** One of the many reforms that resulted from the Second Vatican Council was that the terminology of "last rites" was done away with (in 1973) and the rite of anointing was restored as a rite of prayer for healing at any point when a person faces grave illness. The rite is now called "the anointing of the sick" in the Catholic Church, and it can be performed multiple times.

But I have to tell you that there's a major problem with the Catholic reform of this rite: it just ruins television and movie scenes where a priest is dramatically called to the bedside of a dying Catholic to perform "last rites." For journalists, it ruins the excitement of reporting that "a priest has been called to perform last rites" when a superstar Catholic is seriously ill. When Pope John Paul II was dying in 2005, the press couldn't resist getting out the story that a priest had been called to perform the "last rites" even though the Catholic Church hadn't used that terminology for thirty years.

---

20. In Kittel and Friedrich, *Theological Dictionary of the New Testament*, 1:229–32 (s.v. "ἀλείΦω"). By contrast, words derived from the verb χρίω ("Christ" is one of the words derived from it) carry the sense of anointing for a sacred purpose or office.

What were Catholics thinking about when they messed up the drama of "last rites"? I guess they didn't run it by the marketing department, and they were just thinking about the Scriptures and the pastoral concerns of their parishioners.

Almost all Christian communities practice prayers for healing. They may be offered with more or less formality, and they often involve anointing as a sign of healing. I recall being present at a Pentecostal service in Texas a few years ago. At the conclusion of the service, the pastor asked people to come forward for prayers. A friend of my family who worked as a ceiling installer pulled a vial of oil from his coat pocket and solemnly anointed and prayed over a man who had asked for prayers for healing, a priestly act on the part of an ordinary Christian.

The Life 8: Christian Burial

Christians honor the human body as "the temple of God" (1 Cor 6:19). When a Christian dies, the Christian community traditionally honors the body by returning it to the earth with prayers that look forward to the resurrection of the body. Saint Paul expressed this hope poetically in the first letter to the Corinthians:

OYTWC KAI H ANACTACIC TWN NEKPWN
CΠEIPETAI EN ΦΘΟΡΑ
EΓEIPETAI EN AΦΘΑΡCIA
CΠEIPETAI EN ATIMIA
EΓEIPETAI EN ΔΟΞΗ
CΠEIPETAI EN ACΘENEIA
EΓEIPETAI EN ΔYNAMEI
CΠEIPETAI CWMA ΨYXIKON
EΓEIPETAI CWMA ΠNEYMATIKON

THUS ALSO IS THE RESURRECTION OF THE DEAD
IT IS SOWN WITH CORRUPTION
IT IS RAISED WITH INCORRUPTION
IT IS SOWN IN DISHONOR
IT IS RAISED IN GLORY
IT IS SOWN IN WEAKNESS
IT IS RAISED IN STRENGTH

IT IS SOWN A SOUL BODY
IT IS RAISED A SPIRITUAL BODY

1 Corinthians 15:42–44

Saint Paul said that the resurrection is a "mystery" (verse 51) and the poetic genre is appropriate to the expression of mysteries. Just what is this "spiritual body" with which we are to be raised? Speaking of the resurrection stretches our use of language, just as speaking of God stretches our use of language beyond its normal bounds (chapter 1).

But Paul did not envision the immortality of a disembodied soul. The body is important, and Paul strained the language to say that somehow our bodies will be preserved in the resurrection. Similarly, the literal words of the Apostles' Creed affirm our faith in "the resurrection of the flesh." That can even mean "the meat." However this mystery works out, we look forward to an embodied resurrection.

A Christian funeral is an occasion to bless and celebrate the whole life of a departed sister or brother. A funeral celebration typically includes the following elements:

- **acts of worship** including hymns and prayers

- **reading the Scriptures**, especially Scriptures concerning the resurrection of the dead

- a **homily or sermon** on the Scripture readings

- a **eulogy** or other ways of remembering the deceased (sometimes incorporated into the sermon

- **prayers** on behalf of the community, especially for the family and friends of the deceased

- **prayers to commit the deceased to God** (some Protestant groups do not offer these prayers, believing that the state of the deceased person before God is already settled, and thus prayers for them are pointless),

- a **blessing or invocation**

At the gravesite, the following may also occur:

- reading **brief passages of Scripture**

- a prayer for the **committal of the body to the earth**, typically using the phrase, "ashes to ashes, dust to dust" (Gen 3:19)

- a **blessing**

Although burial was the near-universal custom of Christian communities until quite recently, **cremation** has become an option in recent decades for most Christian groups. The Catholic Church, for example, has allowed cremation since the mid-1960s. Traditionalists worried that the body needed to be preserved so that it could be reconstituted on the day of resurrection. Advocates of cremation maintain that if God is able to reconstitute a body from bones, God can figure out how to reconstitute our bodies from cremated remains. Cremation simply accomplishes in a short span of time what decomposition accomplishes in a longer span of time. In recent decades many Christian churches have built columbaria, areas where cremated remains are kept, with memorial plaques or inscriptions.

A memorial service associated with burial or cremation honors a member of the Christian community, one of the company that the New Testament calls "the saints."[21] In the ages of persecution in the earliest Christian centuries, Christian communities often remembered the death of a martyr on the anniversary of their death. This grew into **the custom of honoring martyrs and other saints on the dates of their deaths, or on a date close by**. I myself was born at the Hospital of St. Therese of Lisieux in Beaumont, Texas, on the (Catholic) feast day of Saint Gregory the Great, who was bishop of Rome around AD 600. Different Christian groups have developed calendars of saints' days, sometimes involving conflicting saints' days.

Some historic Protestant communities have continued the tradition of honoring saints on the dates of their deaths, or on dates close by. The *Book of Common Prayer* of the Episcopal Church in the USA has a calendar of saints' days in which "John and Charles Wesley, Priests" are commemorated on March 3. John Wesley actually died on March 2, 1791, but March 2 was already the feast day for the English saint (bishop and evangelist) Chad of Lichfield, so instead of bumping Saint Chad out of his place on March 2, they took the next available date to honor John Wesley along with his brother Charles.

21. For example, Ephesians 4:12.

The Life 9: Occasional Celebrations

In addition to each of these celebrations, Christian communities have also hallowed the lives of Christians in **occasional celebrations**. Some of these are as follows:

- **infant dedication** (especially in communities that do not practice infant baptism)

- the blessing of churches, homes, and other buildings (even fishing boats!)

- the celebration of **anniversaries** such as birthdays, marriage anniversaries, anniversaries of the deaths of Christians, anniversaries of the founding of congregations, and anniversaries of ordinations or commitments to religious orders

- participation in the blessing of such **life events** as school or university graduations

- blessings and celebrations related to the **agricultural cycles** (for example, harvest celebrations) or particular **vocations**

- blessing of **particular missions** or events in church life

- **recognition of critical spiritual experiences** such as conversion experiences and decisions for Christian vocations

Where allowed, **Christian communities may also participate in civil or public events**, such as prayers for the opening of legislative assemblies, prayers at the inauguration of civic officers, and blessings of public spaces.

At yet another level, Christian communities offer prayers or celebrations whenever occasions arise: prayers for safe travel, for help in times of disasters or crisis, for rain in seasons of drought, and for whatever particular needs arise. The Christian life is a life of feasting and fasting; it is also a life of mourning and celebration, a life marked by consistent praise and prayer.

Sacraments and Mysteries

Chapter 3 has described Christian practices involved in bringing women and men into the Christian community (baptism, teaching the faith, public profession, chrismation or confirmation), and chapter 4 has described practices related to the Lord's Supper. Some of these practices along with the ones described in this chapter have been described as **"sacraments"** or **"mysteries"** in Christian communities. The term "mysteries" is favored by Eastern Christian churches. They typically name seven mysteries (baptism, chrismation, the Divine Liturgy, penance, holy orders, matrimony, and the anointing of the sick), though the number of mysteries is not sharply defined and any privileged moment of contact with the divine can also be described as a "mystery."

The Catholic Church in the late Middle Ages defined seven sacraments as follows:

- baptism
- confirmation
- penance and reconciliation
- the Eucharist
- holy orders
- marriage
- last anointing ("last rites")

As we have seen above, the last was significantly reformed in 1973 and since then has been referred to as the anointing of the sick. Each of these rites has an outward sign and is believed to convey inward grace to those who receive them.

Protestant communities have defined "sacrament" in a more restricted way, limiting sacraments to those acts that a) have outward signs, b) convey inward grace, and c) were instituted by Christ himself with a command that they should be continued.[22] It is this last criterion that limits the number of sacraments for Protestants. For example, prayers for healing are mentioned in the New Testament, but they were not explicitly commanded by Christ himself. In his treatise on *The Babylonian Captivity of the Church* (1520), Martin Luther struggled with whether penance should be included among the sacraments defined in this tighter way. The scriptural basis was from Jesus himself as recorded in John 20:23: "If you forgive the sins of any, they are forgiven them; if you retain the sins of

22. For example, the Catechism of the Church of England defined a sacrament as "an outward and visible sign of an inward and spiritual grace given unto us, ordained by Christ himself" and specified that there are only two sacraments according to this definition (Pelikan and Hotchkiss, *Creeds and Confessions*, 2:369).

any, they are retained." In the end, Luther concluded that the grace given in penance was a reappropriation of the grace that had been initially given in baptism, and thus that penance should not be counted as a separate sacrament.[23]

Luther thus ended up with two sacraments, baptism and the Lord's Supper, and Protestants have generally followed this pattern. But Protestants almost universally practice the other five acts that Catholics consider to be sacraments: confirmation, reconciliation, ordination, marriage, and the anointing of the sick. Penance or reconciliation is not always named as such, but Protestant clergy hear the confessions of persons in their care, counsel them, and may pronounce Christ's forgiveness. Prayers for the sick are not always accompanied by anointing, although liturgical revisions have moved Protestants in recent decades to adopt both formal and informal prayers and services for healing, including the use of anointing. Some Christian communities prefer the term "ordinances" to describe baptism and the Lord's Supper.

The "sacraments," "mysteries," or "ordinances" have a special status in Christian communities, and they're **part of an elaborate cycle of practices and services and simple prayers by which Christian communities bless the lives of their own constituents and sometimes, we hope, bless the lives of those in our wider communities**. In the next chapter, we will turn to practices of individual Christians as they seek the way of Christian holiness.

23. Luther, *Babylonian Captivity of the Church*, the section identified as "the Sacrament of Penance"; in *Three Treatises*, 206–18.

CHAPTER 6

The Path of Self-Giving Love

I WANT TO INVITE you to a deeper Christian faith. Christian communities bless the lives of their members, and enable them by grace to reflect the self-giving love of God. Christians never really grow in isolation from others, but some of the practices of the Christian life are undertaken by Christians alone or in smaller groups of believers. **This chapter describes the way of holiness, the path to reflecting God's inner nature, God's self-giving love, in the lives of Christian disciples.** The way of holiness is a path by which we give ourselves back to God. But before we describe the path of holiness, we have to describe its ugly alternative.

Horror versus Holiness

Christians live in the real world, the good world God created, and the world in which God became a human for us. But it is also the world in which people starve to death, are terrified and raped and murdered and succumb to memory-erasing diseases and dependencies and cancers and a thousand more plagues. We don't have the option of believing in God apart from the horrors with which we live. We do have the option of believing that **these horrors are not what God intends.** Traditional Christian communities believe that there are terrifying powers at work in our world that thwart God's purposes.

The horrors we're talking about now are what we traditionally call sin and evil.[1] If the word "sin" offends you (dear tender soul) then maybe you can think up a less offensive term. You'll just have to live with the fact that your whatever-you-call-it looks suspiciously similar to my sin. We could consider using "corruption" as a not-quite-precise equivalent to the term "sin." "Corruption" does have a few advantages over the word "sin." At least in my formation as a young man, I came to associate "sin" with a rather small list of personal foibles, basically any failure to follow the code of morality that said, "Don't drink, don't smoke, don't chew, and don't go with the girls that do." Stuff like that—that was sin and evil.

But the Jewish and Christian Scriptures speak of sin and evil as something far more hideous and universal than the private screw-ups of individual people. In the eighth chapter of his letter to the Romans, Saint Paul wrote,

> For the creation waits with eager longing for the revealing of the children of God; for the creation was subjected to futility, not of its own will, but by the will of the one who subjected it, in hope that the creation itself will be set free from its bondage to decay and will obtain the freedom of the glory of the children of God. (Rom 8:19–21)

Sin and evil have a cosmic character: "bondage to decay" infects the entire creation. In this sense, sin is the overarching screwed-up-ness of a world that can allow such a thing to happen as a child starving when food rots away in storehouses.

Don't believe in sin? Take your pick: read the Bible or the news feeds. You'll get it either way. You can still call it what you want—just don't let it sound trivial when we're talking about rape and murder and starvation in a world where there's food. Christians traditionally call it sin.[2]

---

1. Sin and evil as a presupposition of teaching about Christian salvation are discussed in the "Joint Declaration on the Doctrine of Justification" affirmed by the Lutheran World Federation and the Catholic Church (1999), and subsequently affirmed by the World Methodist Council (2006), ¶¶ 19–21 (see Pelikan and Hotchkiss, *Creeds and Confessions*, 882).

2. In comparison to this section of *A Deeper Christian Faith*, see the section "Sin According to Sacred Law" in Joint Commission of Churches in Turkey, *Christianity* (40–41).

The Path of Self-Giving Love

ΟΥ ΓΑΡ ΕCΤΙΝ ΔΙΑCΤΟΛΗ
ΠΑΝΤΕC ΓΑΡ ΗΜΑΡΤΟΝ
ΚΑΙ ΥCΤΕΡΟΥΝΤΑΙ ΤΗC ΔΟΞΗC ΤΟΥ ΘΕΟΥ

FOR THERE IS NO DISTINCTION
FOR ALL HAVE SINNED
AND FALL SHORT OF THE GLORY OF GOD

Romans 3:22–23

Let me say a word on behalf of sin. It's a real democracy, an equal-opportunity employer, a fraternity with abysmally low standards of admission, excellent diversity, and thoroughgoing inclusivity. So who killed Jesus Christ? Blame it on the Romans! Blame it on the Jews! But when we finish trying to pin the blame on someone else, this is what we sing:

> Who was the guilty? Who brought this upon thee?
> Alas, my treason, Jesus, hath undone thee!
> 'Twas I, Lord Jesus, I it was denied thee;
> I crucified thee.[3]

I think that that old Lutheran hymn means that the murderer of Jesus Christ is the author of this book. And you're very welcome to my company! We need help, and I mean badly. So is there any hope? "Who will rescue me from this body of death" (Rom 7:24)?

You probably know the beginning of the answer. The beginning of the answer is divine help or grace made possible by the work of Jesus Christ. But there's more: not only does God offer us help, but God offers us proof. The proof is **a company of people, in heaven and now on earth, who reflect the glory and the holiness of God. We call them saints. The mirror opposite of the horror of sin and evil is holiness or saintliness**. A saint is a person who reflects the holiness of God. The saints are the living testimony, the living evidence on earth that the way of evil does not prevail.

Now don't believe all the hype you hear. You might not guess this from looking at the pictures with the harps and the halos—those were sent out by the Saint Marketing Department—but the truth is that saints are bad people and they often have bad teeth and bad breath to boot. Here's how a saint prays about sexual temptation: "Give me chastity and self-control, but,

---

3. Heermann, "Hertzliebster Jesu," translated by Robert S. Bridges, cited from United Methodist Church, *United Methodist Hymnal*, 289.

er, not right now" (Saint Augustine of Hippo).[4] Maybe that was BC (before Augustine's conversion), but give the man some credit for honesty.

Some of the saints were as bad as Augustine, some were even as bad as I am, and I don't just mean that they started out as bad people and then ended up as goody-goody nice people. I don't expect to end up that way. What I mean is that God made them saints in spite of their massive and persistent human flaws. **God made them saints in spite of themselves**. It's a very reassuring thought. So are you bad enough to be a saint? **God doesn't make saints from anything but sinners**.

Grace: The Antidote to the Horror of Sin and Evil

Grace is the divine antidote to the horror of sin and evil. It means help. It means the power to do what we can't do on our own, a power that comes from outside of ourselves.

TH ΓΑΡ ΧΑΡΙΤΙ ΕϹΤΕ ϹΕϹШϹΜΕΝΟΙ
ΔΙΑ ΠΙϹΤΕШϹ
ΚΑΙ ΤΟΥΤΟ ΟΥΚ ΕΞ ΥΜШΝ
ΘΕΟΥ ΤΟ ΔШΡΟΝ

FOR BY GRACE YOU HAVE BEEN SAVED
THROUGH FAITH
AND THIS IS NOT OF YOURSELVES
IT IS THE GIFT OF GOD

Ephesians 2:8

Repentance, grace, and faith are tightly bound together. **Repentance** means we acknowledge what we cannot do, that we need help from someone else. **Grace** is the help that comes from someone else. **Faith** means that we have to trust the other one whose help will enable us to do what we cannot do.[5]

But once again we have to note the terrible failure of standard English in translating this passage. It does not say that "you" as an individual have

4. Augustine, *Conf.* 8:7; in Augustine, *Confessions*, 14:44; my own somewhat-free translation.

5. See "Joint Declaration on the Doctrine of Justification," ¶¶ 19–21 and 25–27, in Pelikan and Hotchkiss, *Creeds and Confessions*, 882–84.

been saved or delivered or helped. Paul could have written that, but he did not. What Paul wrote was that "you" as a group (plural) "have been saved by grace through faith, and this is not your [again plural] work, it is God's gift." If I can express it in my native dialect, "For by grace y'all have been saved through faith, and this is not from y'all's selves, it is the gift of God." Something like that. It's about being helped together, as a group or a community. Grace does what we can't do. That's why we sing about "Amazing Grace."

The Path 1: Repentance

So what to do first? As noted in chapter 3 about becoming a Christian, the first step on the path of holiness is to admit we have a problem. We definitely have a problem. Repentance means admitting we have a problem and—this may be even more important—admitting we need help. Earlier we discussed repentance as our first acknowledgement that we need help. In this chapter, we're saying that **repentance has to continue**. It is **a continual "habit,"** like something you wear, the continual attitude of a believer who knows that we still stand in desperate need of help from beyond ourselves.

דרשו יהוה בהמצאו

קראהו בהיותו קרוב

SEEK יהוה WHILE HE MAY BE FOUND
CALL UPON HIM WHILE HE IS NEAR

Isaiah 55:6

Repentance means calling on God for help. There's a tendency to think that repentance just means listing our sins with an official acknowledgment of regret. "Dear God, I deeply regret to inform you, but I coveted my neighbor's new car. Oh yeah, and that's not all I coveted. But hey, listen, I did not covet his house, and my neighbor does not have cows or monkeys or oxen or donkeys or maidservants or manservants to covet [Exodus 20:17 and parallels]. And don't you already know all this stuff?"

The correct answer is yes, God already knows this stuff, even the extent to which we may or may not regret it. **Repentance means** more than listing sins with an indication of regret. It means **calling out for help**. That's different. Calling out for help means we intend to change, we expect to change, we ask for help to change. Now we're getting somewhere.

I wish I could tell you that repentance is just a private matter between you and God. It is that, but not just that. Think about it like this: God has put other people around us to help us. So **if we really need help, we need to say it**. Out loud. In the presence of people who can keep secrets and who just might be able to help us find the help we need. We may need formal ways of admitting our failures and our need for grace (see the section of the last chapter on "Repentance, Confession, and the Pronouncement of Forgiveness"). We may also need circles of accountability, groups of Christian friends to whom we can admit our need for grace (see the subsequent section "Saints and Sinners: All Together Now").

The Path 2: Commandments and Promises

One of the things we can't do by ourselves is keep God's commandments. We need help. Christians in the past have sometimes maligned Jews by saying that Jews think they can keep the commandments without any help of grace. Ask any well-instructed Jew and they'll tell you that *Torah*, God's law, is pure grace. Watch how Jews reverence the Torah scroll when it is brought out of the ark in a synagogue service. Their joy says, "This is grace." We all need extra help, grace, to keep God's commandments.

At Oxford University, the story is told of a stern Protestant evangelical who became a university faculty member in the Victorian era. A college servant offered him wine in the Senior Commons Room after dinner, saying, "Would you like wine, sir?"

"Sir," replied the Protestant with a stern look, "I would as soon commit adultery as drink wine."

The servant thought for a moment, then replied, "Most of us would, sir."

Most of us would. We need help. But through grace, the commandments become promises. The commandment "You shall not steal," with grace, becomes the promise "You will not steal."[6]

---

6. The insight that commandments become promises through grace is from John Wesley, for example, in his sermon "Upon Our Lord's Sermon on the Mount, Discourse V," 2:3; in Wesley, *Sermons*, 1:554–55, where he states that "every command in holy writ is only a covered promise."

The Ten Commandments given in Exodus 20:1–7 and Deuteronomy 5:6–21 have been a foundation of Jewish and Christian morality. Although Christians and Jews agree that these passages from Exodus and Deuteronomy contain the Commandments, they differ on exactly how the Bible verses should be divided into ten separate commandments. Catholics and Lutherans have one way of dividing the text; Eastern Orthodox, Reformed, Anglican, and other Christians divide them a different way. A summary of the commandments as they are divided up by Eastern Orthodox, Reformed, Anglican, and Methodist churches is as follows:

I. I am the Lord your God who brought you out of bondage. You shall have no other gods but me.

II. You shall not make for yourself any idol.

III. You shall not invoke with malice the Name of the Lord your God.

IV. Remember the Sabbath day and keep it holy.

V. Honor your father and your mother.

VI. You shall not commit murder.

VII. You shall not commit adultery.

VIII. You shall not steal.

IX. You shall not be a false witness.

X. You shall not covet anything that belongs to your neighbor.[7]

Jesus regarded the disposition of the heart as the real issue involved in violation of the commandments. "But I say to you that everyone who looks at a woman with lust has already committed adultery with her in his heart" (Matt 5:28 and parallels). Maybe that's why there's one commandment (VII) that says not to commit adultery, and then a further commandment (X) that says not to covet one's neighbor's wife (Exod 20:17 and parallels).[8]

If we're going to avoid not only violating these commandments, but also avoid the *desire* to violate the commandments, **it's going to take a**

7. This summary is derived from the liturgical form of the Ten Commandments given in the Episcopal Church, *Book of Common Prayer*, 350. See the liturgical form in the appendix to this book below.

8. In comparison to this section of *A Deeper Christian Faith*, see the section "The Application of Love in Christianity" in Joint Commission of Churches in Turkey, *Christianity*, 80–82.

lot of grace. A whole lot of grace. It's going to take grace that can change what we desire, grace that can change commandments into promises. But **this is what the saints have claimed: grace happens. They come to desire what God desires**. And what they claim is that when they desire what God desires, they're truly happy. I'm a long way from there, but I'm looking forward to it. Grace is available; start by asking.

The Path 3: The Habit of Prayer

We need grace, and grace leads to grace, "grace upon grace" (John 1:16). Grace leads us to certain habits that open up channels of grace for us. The word **"habit"** comes from a Latin word, *habitus*, that meant something you wear, like a robe. A "habit" has come to mean something that we do so regularly that it's like something we wear. There are **three habits that are consistently practiced by those who need grace badly**. One is the habit of **being formed by the Scriptures**. Another is the habit of **fasting**, abstaining from food, or at least from rich foods, for particular periods. The third is the habit of regular, daily **prayer**.

Here's a verse from the book of *Tehillim*, or Psalms, describing a regular practice of prayer:

שבע ביום הללתיך על משפטי צדקך

SEVEN TIMES A DAY I PRAISE YOU
FOR YOUR RIGHTEOUS ORDINANCES

Psalm 119:164

This verse did not prescribe a formal practice; it simply meant that worshipers offered prayers of praise frequently through the day. From very ancient times, Jews had recited the *Shema* (see chapter 1) every morning and evening, following the injunction that these words should be said "when you lie down and when you rise up" (Deut 6:7). When Jews were exiled to Babylon, they developed the custom of praying at certain times in the day, and they seem to have imported this practice back into the temple when they returned to Jerusalem before the time of Jesus.

The book of the Acts of the Apostles records that "Peter and John went up to the temple at the hour of prayer, the ninth hour" (Acts 3:1), that is, at mid-afternoon. The Acts of the Apostles also describes Christians praying at mid-morning ("the third hour of the day," Acts 2:15) and at mid-day ("the sixth hour of the day," Acts 10:3, 9). It appears that Christians regularly prayed at the specific times of the day at roughly three-hour intervals that had become customary for Jews. In this way, we can understand the statement in Acts 2:42, which says that the first Christian disciples continued in "the apostles' teaching and fellowship, in the breaking of bread, and in **the prayers**" (my emphasis). Some translations simply render this as "prayers," but the definite article ("the") indicates an established practice that readers of the Acts would have understood.

As practices of daily prayer evolved in Christian communities, these three times of prayer, along with waking up, sunrise, sunset, and going to sleep, formed a cycle of seven daily times for prayer. Traditional names have been attached to these times of prayer as follows:

- waking ("lauds")
- sunrise ("prime")
- mid-morning ("terce")
- noon ("sext")
- mid-afternoon ("none," pronounced *nohn*)
- sunset ("vespers")
- going to bed ("compline")

Variations on these hours of prayer were observed by monastic communities in Eastern as well as Western Christian churches, and many Christian leaders outside of monastic communities also observed the hours of prayer. **The Muslim practice of formal prayer** (*salāt*) at five specific times of the day governed by the position of the sun continues these early-Christian customs of prayer through the day. Muslims succeeded in making this a very common practice; it is considered to be one of the "Five Pillars" of Sunni Islam.[9]

Very few ordinary Christians took up the practice of the hours of prayer. They probably knew the Lord's Prayer and perhaps a few other texts from the service for the Lord's Supper that they had memorized, and they could add their own prayers to these. At the time of the reformations, **Luther** suggested that Christians every morning and evening should make a

9. On Muslim observance of *salāt*, see Ayoub, *Islam*, 56–59.

sign of the cross, say the Lord's Prayer and the Apostles' Creed, and then a special prayer appropriate to the morning or the evening.[10]

The Church of England arranged the most important parts of the services of the prayer hours into two daily services, **morning and evening prayer**, in *The Book of Common Prayer*. These services are not only performed in English churches and cathedrals, but they are also read in private homes for family morning and evening prayers. English-speaking Christianity has been deeply formed by the prayer book liturgies for morning and evening prayer, though they suffer from Anglicans' penchant for seemingly endless canticles, which are totally cool if you have a choir of boys to sing them in a beautiful echoing cathedral, but can lead to death by boredom as a practice of daily private devotion.

From around the 1700s AD, many Protestants took up **the practice of extempore prayer**. That means prayers that we just make up on the spot. This practice reflects the growth of Protestant movements that emphasized the role of the heart and the affections in religious life. Extempore prayers were understood as being more genuine expressions of one's personal feelings than formal or written prayers could be. At first, extempore prayers were offered in addition to formal prayers. In preparing a version of the *Book of Common Prayer* for his followers, for example, the evangelist John Wesley urged them in 1784 to use the prescribed services "on the Lord's Day, in all their congregations, reading the litany only on Wednesdays and Fridays, and praying extempore on all other days."[11]

Most of us who have been part of Christian communities that practice extempore prayer know that extempore prayers can in fact become formulaic very quickly. Certain patterns are taken up ("Jesus, we just pray that . . .") and repeated, and these come to have a ritual character. So perhaps it's best to acknowledge that there should be both informal (extempore) prayer as well as formal structures of prayer. Written, formal prayers allow us to pray with our ancestors in the faith when we use the words they used to address God. Contemporary prayers, including extempore prayers, allow us to speak to God of our own immediate concerns.

Whether formal or extempore, spoken out loud or expressed only in our thoughts, one of the challenges in Christian prayer involves **the twofold**

10. See Luther's *Small Catechism*, section 7, on "Morning and Evening Prayers"; in Pelikan and Hotchkiss, *Creeds and Confessions*, 2:44.

11. See letter of John Wesley's "To Dr. Coke, Mr. Asbury, and Our Brethren in North America," dated September 10, 1784; in John and Charles Wesley, *Wesley Reader*, 195.

movement of 1) being honest with God in our prayers and 2) being open to God in our prayers. One of the genuine problems inherent in formal or written prayers is that they are typically chosen because they reflect Christian piety, but for this very reason they can give the impression that we just pray the nice things that we think God wants to hear from us. We have to come to the point in our prayers where we can express to God our joys, our hopes, our ambitions, our disappointments, our frustrations, our anger, including our anger against God, and our many desires—yes, even the ones that might be considered "unholy" or not-so-nice desires. God, after all, knows these things. There's a big problem with being polite when you pray. Niceness or politeness in prayer can amount to self-deception before God. The Psalms, when read in their entirety and with the eyes of the understanding wide open, give us language to express some less-than-holy things that we really need to say before God.

The other movement in prayer is **the movement in which we make ourselves open to God**, time to shut up our mouthing and listen for a while. Kind of. "Listen" may not be just the right word. Maybe it's better to say that **we make ourselves open to be formed or shaped by God in prayer.** The saints say—and I have to admit that this is way out of my league—that the ultimate goal of prayer is simply to be with God in such a way that we enjoy each other's company without the need for a lot of chatter. If you've been away from someone you love, you chatter away at first, filling each other in about what's been going on. And then you just want to be with each other. Just sit still. And be with each other. And that's **the goal to which prayer is ultimately directed: simply to be in the presence of God.**

The Path 4: The Habit of Being Formed by the Scriptures

A second habit instilled by grace and opening up streams of grace is the habit of being formed by the Scriptures. Saint Justin Martyr described the worship of the Roman Christian community in the 150s AD, and one element of the worship he described was that "the memoirs of the apostles or the writings of the prophets are read" (see chapter 4).[12] The weekly reading from the Old or New Testaments may have been all the exposure that ordinary Christians had to the Scriptures, since manuscripts were very

---

12. Justin Martyr, *1 Apol.* 67:1–5; in Justin Martyr, *Justin, Philosopher and Martyr*, 258 and 260 (text), 259 and 261 (translation).

precious. Whole congregations may have had only a few books or excerpts of what we consider to be the Christian Bible today.

It's difficult to find passages in the New Testament that refer to the New Testament itself. The New Testament hadn't been organized or recognized as a single collection in the decades when its books were being written. When New Testament writings refer to the "Scriptures" (John 5:39; 1 Cor 15:3–4; 2 Tim 3:16), they almost inevitably refer to the Hebrew and Aramaic Scriptures that we call the Old Testament. **Only a few passages hint at the authority ascribed to New Testament writings.** Here's one such passage from the second letter to the Thessalonians:

ΑΡΑ ΟΥΝ ΑΔΕΛΦΟΙ ϹΤΗΚΕΤΕ
ΚΑΙ ΚΡΑΤΕΙΤΕ ΤΑϹ ΠΑΡΑΔΟϹΕΙϹ
ΑϹ ΕΔΙΔΑΧΘΗΤΕ
ΕΙΤΕ ΔΙΑ ΛΟΓΟΥ
ΕΙΤΕ ΔΙ ΕΠΙϹΤΟΛΗϹ ΗΜΩΝ

SO THEN BROTHERS AND SISTERS STAND FAST
AND HOLD ON TO THE TRADITIONS
THAT YOU WERE TAUGHT
EITHER BY WORD OR BY OUR LETTER

2 Thessalonians 2:15

In this exhortation, the author gives equal credence to oral traditions ("by word") and to written works ("by our letter"). We have considered in chapters 2 and 4 instances of oral traditions embedded in 1 Corinthians 11:23–26 and 15:1–4. These are not references to the authority of the New Testament as later defined—that is, the twenty-seven books we now recognize as New Testament Scriptures—but to the authority of the letters sent by this author to the Thessalonians. By the middle of the 100s AD, a loosely-defined group of books, including most of the ones we recognize as the New Testament, was used in proto-orthodox Christian communities. By the middle of the 300s AD, Christian communities had largely recognized the New Testament as we have it today (see chapter 2).

We have to recognize, then, that **Christians were formed by oral traditions and by the oral hearing of the Scriptures in the early centuries.** When they encountered the Scriptures, for example, in hearing the Jewish or Christian Scriptures read at the celebration of the Supper, their encounter was overwhelmingly an oral encounter with the texts. Only a few leaders were able to handle written texts of the Christian Scriptures and to read them. Most had to rely on their memories of biblical texts.

Christian monastic communities from the 300s AD instituted **ways of reading the Scriptures in regular, daily cycles**. Benedictine houses developed the custom of reading the whole book of Psalms every week, along with other Scriptures recited at the hours of prayer and in sessions of recitation. Their habit was to recite the Scriptures slowly so that monks could remember and meditate on them. This way of reading and hearing the Bible came to be called *lectio divina*, "divine reading." Monks with no ability to read could develop a huge knowledge of biblical texts in this way. The goal of *lectio divina* was to form the monks spiritually by their hearing of and meditation on the Scriptures.

The Protestant and Catholic reformations arose in the decades just after the invention of the modern printing press, and they flourished in a time of growing literacy among middle-class European people. This had a huge effect on **the devotional use of the Scriptures as Bibles eventually became available to ordinary folks**. Both Catholic and Protestant churches sponsored modern-language translations of the Bible. Protestants sometimes accused Catholics of suppressing modern translations, but as you might guess, it was the Protestant-authorized translations that Catholic states were concerned to suppress, and Protestant states returned the favor by suppressing Catholic-authorized translations.

Despite these efforts at suppression, the Scriptures were widely available in modern translations from the 1600s. **From this time, personal reading of the Bible became one of the central habits by which ordinary Christians sought to be formed spiritually**. Two general patterns emerged. Anglican and Lutheran churches and the Catholic Church favored **the reading of the Scriptures in the sequence of the Christian year focused on the life of Christ** (see chapter 2). They developed lectionaries, lists of weekly and daily readings, following the liturgical calendar. The *Book of Common Prayer* of the Church of England included a Psalter with the entire book of Psalms divided into thirty daily sections so that it could be read each month. The other pattern that prevailed in Reformed churches and then in evangelical Protestant communities was **the sequential reading of the Bible, or at least of particular books within the Bible, not synchronized with a liturgical calendar**.

Reading the Bible today is not the same as it was for our ancestors. Two or more centuries of critical studies of the Christian and Jewish Scriptures have raised multiple questions about the origins of the biblical texts, their accuracy with respect to the events they describe, the multiple sources on which they were based, and the ways in which the Scriptures have been changed through copying, translation, and particular cultural understandings. Those of us who have taken seriously the challenges that these studies pose find it difficult to revert to a naïve reading of the Scriptures, as if they were simply words that God dictated to human authors acting as secretaries for the divine. The Scriptures themselves hardly allow that understanding, except in the case of a few specific prophetic utterances.

Critical studies may challenge us, but they **can also reveal depths of understanding that eluded simpler readings of the Bible**. Understanding how Paul "received" and "handed on" the gospel message and the practice of the Lord's Supper, for example, gives us a sense of the immense importance of the gospel and the Supper, and a sense of how very old those narratives are (1 Cor 15:1–4; 11:23–26) in relation to the writings of the New Testament (see chapter 2). **One must not fall into the naïve presupposition that a critical study of the Scriptures will automatically generate unorthodox conclusions**, or that any unorthodox conclusion is bound to be a more adequate understanding of the Bible than the ways in which Christian communities have historically understood the Scriptures.

It's also important to say that **devotional biblical study does not simply have to mean reading biblical texts**. Most of us have been shaped by the "Gutenberg galaxy," the modern culture in which we encounter texts as printed documents either in bound books or in electronic versions of the texts.[13] We need to remember that Jews and Christians first experienced these texts as oral texts. Even the texts that were written down were experienced by most Christian and Jews as they were read aloud. We also need to remember that none of these texts were written in English, and none of them had punctuation marks or upper- and lowercase letters. They looked and sounded very different than a modern reading can provide.

Translations that render biblical texts in airy, fresh, contemporary-sounding English convey multiple misunderstandings—most problematically, they convey to readers the false impression that the world of the ancient texts was very much like our own world. There's an Italian saying, *traduttore traditore*, "a translator is a traitor." That's why **it's important to see texts and to hear them in the ancient languages**. Even if we don't

13. McLuhan, *Gutenberg Galaxy*.

understand the language, we can sense that they're embedded in a world very alien from our own. We have to encounter the texts, not by forcing them into our world, but by allowing ourselves to enter into their world.

Even with critical study, it's possible to enjoy the narratives and poetry and letters and other literature included in the sacred Scriptures. I once heard a lecture in Oxford by a distinguished professor of the Old Testament. He described the stories of the Hebrew patriarchs in the early chapters of Genesis, giving elaborate reflections on how varied strands of traditions had been woven together into the narratives we read in Genesis. After the lecture, I asked him if that's how he thought about these texts when he heard them read aloud in church. He said no, that when he heard them in church, he simply enjoyed the stories.

One key to reading the Bible faithfully is keeping ourselves open to the possibility that it will change us. That means that we keep ourselves open to critical understandings of the Bible, and we also keep ourselves open to the present work of the Holy Spirit, inspiring us today as the Holy Spirit inspired people in ages past to write down the texts of the Scriptures and to read and interpret them in Jewish and Christian communities. If we read the Scriptures hoping that they will confirm our presumptions or prejudices, we are not likely to be changed by them. We have to listen to the Scriptures, to read them and study them, expecting to be shaped by them and through them and by God.

The Path 5: The Habit of Fasting

A third spiritual practice that forms Christians is **the habit of deliberately abstaining from food for particular times, the habit of fasting.** Jesus himself spoke of fasting as a common religious practice and warned against fasting in such a way that we make a show of our piety:

ⲞⲦⲀⲚ ⲆⲈ ⲚⲎⲤⲦⲈⲨⲎⲦⲈ
ⲘⲎ ⲄⲒⲚⲈⲤⲐⲈ ⲰⲤ ⲞⲒ ⲨⲠⲞⲔⲢⲒⲦⲀⲒ
ⲤⲔⲨⲐⲢⲰⲠⲞⲒ

AND WHEN YOU FAST
DO NOT BECOME LIKE HYPOCRITES
WITH GLOOMY FACES

Matthew 6:16

Those who practice fasting know that it can be a transformative practice, but not for the reasons you might guess. When you fast, you wash your face and get on with your business. It's not for showing off. **The idea really is not that we please God by making ourselves feel miserable**.

Could I convince you that when you're not fasting, you are, in a sense, drugged? Moderate fasting is a very natural practice. It really means a return to a primitive and almost universal human condition, the condition of being slightly hungry. This is a weird condition only for modern people accustomed to having food available and consuming it whenever they want. So, odd as it may seem, **fasting can feel like a return to reality**, a return to the way humans have existed for centuries in the past. When we fast, we realize that our so-called "normal" lives are drugged lives, drugged by the amounts of substances we consume, and drugged by the regularity with which we consume them. I am not making this up: after practicing fasting for a while, in moderation, it comes to feel like a return to normalcy after being drugged or intoxicated.

Unlike the disciplines of prayer and biblical study, **fasting has some specific dangers associated with it**. It can become tied up with low self-esteem and eating disorders, and inappropriate fasting can be dangerous for bodily and mental health. That kind of fasting does not honor God. So let me offer you some of the standard warnings and advices about fasting.

- First, **abstaining from food completely for a few hours is not for everyone**. If you feel seriously hungry or you can't function normally, don't do it. Smaller people may not be able to sustain regular activities without more consistent food, and those with medical conditions like diabetes may not be able to control blood glucose levels without regular food. A traditional alternative practiced by Christians is **abstention**, to take regular food but abstain from sweet foods or rich foods for particular periods.

- **Fast moderately**. The early Christian writer Tertullian, writing in Northern Africa around AD 200, explained that the weekly fasts of Christians extended from the time they woke up until midafternoon.[14]

14 Tertullian, *De Ieiunio* 14; in *Corpus Christianorum Series Latina II*, 2:1272–73. Tertullian here uses the term *stationes* ("stations") to refer to fasts from sunrise to the ninth hour of the day.

Similarly, the eighteenth-century evangelist John Wesley fasted from the time he woke up until teatime.[15] That's not a severe fast.

- **Do take water when you fast.** Hydration is important to allow your body to function normally. I also take my usual coffee in the morning. If I don't, I know I'll have headaches. I take my regular medications as well, and one of my pills requires that I eat a just little bit with it, like a few nuts and raisins, or else it will cause an upset stomach.

- **Brush your teeth** regularly and consider using a mouthwash if you're around others. Fasting can cause bad breath. I have already said that saints can have bad breath. Saints can also brush their teeth. Consider it an act of Christian hospitality.

- **Break your fast carefully.** Start with some dried fruits and nuts, for example, before you eat rich food.

The idea is not to make yourself miserable, but to become spiritually aware by abstaining from regular food.

One of the interesting effects of fasting is **heightened senses**. This was perhaps the most surprising thing I discovered about fasting the first time I tried it. Of course, this means that we're more sensitive to taste and smell when we're slightly hungry, but it also seems to bring about a broader heightened awareness of things going on. Maybe this is due to the simple fact that we've changed our routine and we experience the stuff we experience every day from a different perspective. However it works, fasting entails a greater sense of what's happening around us. It lets us break loose, just for a little space, from constant and usually unnoticed habits that accompany our daily routines. It can free us to perceive God more clearly in the things we do from hour to hour.

As indicated above, there have been **certain times when Christians fasted** from the earliest Christian centuries. The advantage of observing shared times of fasting is that we can engage in it along with others, not just by ourselves. Christians historically observed **Wednesdays and Fridays** of every week as "**half-fasts**," meaning that the period of fasting lasted only from the time one awoke until mid-afternoon, roughly 3:00 p.m.[16] The season of **Lent**, eventually a forty-day period extending from Ash Wednesday through the day before Easter, **involved a longer fast from rising in the morning until sunset**, but Christians broke their fasts by eating regular

15. Heitzenrater, *Wesley and the People*, 49–50.
16. Tertullian, *De Ieiunio* 14, in *Corpus Christianorum Series Latina II*, 2:1272–73.

food at the conclusion of these occasions, late in the afternoon for the Wednesday and Friday fasts, and after sunset for the Lenten fast.[17] The Muslim observance of the fast of Ramadān seems to be patterned after the early Christian Lenten fast.[18]

I've heard sermons about how we're supposed to fast with the right motivations. For example, you're not supposed to be fasting just to lose weight. Perhaps it's problematic if fasting is just a religious excuse to accomplish something entirely different. Perhaps. But I'm not sure I buy the argument about getting our motives straight, especially if it means you don't fast because you don't "feel like it." I never really feel like it, and I'm not sure if I ever have the right motivations. If I were to shed a pound or two as a result of fasting, I suspect the Holy One would not be particularly offended. **Motivations are overrated, so just do it.** Worry about the motivations later. Or not.

I have said above that moderate fasting brings about a normal human state, a state in which we are more aware of our tendency to consume, and more aware of our need for God, the hunger for God's righteousness. There are other reasons for fasting. Sometimes it's **an appropriate expression of sadness**, like the times when you have heard terrible news and you just naturally don't feel like eating. Sometimes fasting is an appropriate expression of a whole community's sadness over a turn of events. In some cases, a fast may mark a special occasion, often in **preparation for a special mission**. Or maybe, just in **preparation for a feast**.

And this brings us back around to something we touched on in chapter 4. The Christian life is not bologna sandwiches every day. It is a life of fasting and of feasting. Even during the season of Lent, Christians following historic traditions are obliged to observe Sundays as feasts to celebrate the resurrection of Jesus Christ.

Want a deeper Christian faith? You need to fast. You need to feast. Think of these as holy obligations. Have some bread. Have some wine. It's good. It's really good after you've fasted for a while.

---

17. The forty-day period of Lent (*quadragesima*) is referred to in canon 5 of the Council of Nicea; in Tanner, *Decrees of the Ecumenical Councils*, 1:8.

18. On Muslim observance of the fast of Ramadān in general, see Ayoub, *Islam*, 60–63.

The Path 6: Experiences of the Divine

Fasting can make us more sensitive to a wide range of experiences, including religious ones. Many of the saints describe particular religious experiences on the path of holiness—some vivid and dramatic, others less so. We have seen above (chapter 1) that religious experiences are not unusual, even among people who do not think of themselves as traditionally religious. The process of coming to authentic faith in Christ, what we have called conversion (chapter 3), sometimes involves dramatic religious experiences. Beyond the generic religious experiences common to almost everyone and particular experiences associated with Christian conversion, believers have described some religious experiences as signposts on the way to holiness.

Leaders of Christian monastic communities in both the Eastern and Western Christian churches elaborated teachings about a process of cleansing the soul through prayer, fasting, and meditation that would lead to an experience of union or oneness with God. They sometimes described three stages in this process:

- **Purgation**, a process in which God's grace leads the soul by way of fasting and prayer and meditation to dissociate itself from destructive passions that lead to outward sins;

- **Illumination**, in which God's grace enables the soul to be more and more filled with love for God, for humanity, and for God's creation; and finally

- **Union**, in which the soul resides or rests in unity with God.

In Eastern Christian traditions, this goal of union with God was sometimes described as seeing God "with the eyes of the flesh." As Moses could not see God's face but was allowed to see God's trailing "glory" (Exod 33:18–23), Eastern Christian teachers maintained that the "eyes of the flesh" cannot see God directly, but through a special gift of grace, they can be enabled to see God's glory.

Not all Christians could participate in the lifelong process that monastic leaders envisioned. But ordinary Christians in Catholic and Orthodox traditions did have dramatic Christian experiences, sometimes visionary experiences. For example, a Native American who had been baptized as Juan Diego saw a series of visions of the Blessed Virgin Mary at Tepeyac near present-day Mexico City in December 1531. He saw Mary in a particular iconic form known from earlier Spanish Catholicism as "the Virgin of Guadalupe," and his experiences as well as the image of the Virgin of Guadalupe are celebrated as the roots of popular Mexican Catholicism. Juan Diego is just one example of ordinary Christians celebrated among the saints in Orthodox and Catholic church life.

Protestant Christians have also claimed experiences of God. Some Protestant groups have valued particular forms of religious experiences. Methodist and Holiness communities have encouraged believers to seek **entire sanctification**, which Methodist leader John Wesley envisioned as the fulfillment of the Great Commandment to love God with all our being. These communities have taught that by God's grace it is possible to love God completely, and members of these Christian communities have testified to an experience in which they felt assured by God that by grace they had come to complete love for God. Holiness churches maintain that such an experience should be a normative expectation of Christian believers.[19]

In some Methodist and Holiness church circles, the experience of entire sanctification was described as "the baptism of the Holy Spirit," seeing the experience of the apostles on the day of Pentecost as an experience of entire sanctification. But around the very late 1800s and the early 1900s, some teachers began to describe "the baptism of the Holy Spirit" as a separate experience following conversion and entire sanctification. Their belief was that **the baptism of the Holy Spirit** was a special empowerment of the Spirit accompanied by the evidence of speaking in unknown tongues, as described in the biblical account of the day of Pentecost (Acts 2:4). This sense of the baptism of the Holy Spirit has been a central, defining feature of modern Pentecostalism. Doctrinal confessions of Pentecostal churches describe it as a normative part of Christian experience after conversion,[20] though many if not most Pentecostal churches no longer teach or emphasize an experience of entire sanctification separate from conversion and the baptism of the Holy Spirit.

Saints and Sinners: All Together Now

Many of the practices described in this chapter can be carried out by ourselves apart from a community. But these practices can be strengthened by

19. Church of the Nazarene, Articles of Faith (1908), 10; in Pelikan and Hotchkiss, *Creeds and Confessions*, 3:412.

20. Assemblies of God, "Statement of Fundamental Truths" (1916), items 5 and 6; in Pelikan and Hotchkiss, *Creeds and Confessions*, 3:428.

a small group that holds us accountable for our actions and our behaviors. The letter to the Ephesians envisions a Christian community as being subject to one another:

ΥΠΟΤΑϹϹΟΜΕΝΟΙ ΑΛΛΗΛΟΙϹ
ΕΝ ΦΟΒⲰ ΧΡΙϹΤΟΥ

ΒΕ SUBJECT TO ONE ANOTHER
IN FEAR OF CHRIST

Ephesians 5:21

The passage goes on to explain this with respect to roles in an ancient household: wives and husbands, children and fathers, slaves and masters should all "be subject to one other in fear of Christ" (Eph 5:21—6:9).[21]

This is how Christian communities function for their members. **We look out for each other.** Early Christian monastic communities functioned to "watch over each other" as Christians. By the 1200s, some monastic communities had made provisions for "third orders" that allowed married persons to keep some of the rules of their communities. But this is not just a Catholic thing. Many Baptist congregations state in their church covenants their commitment to "watch over one another in brotherly love."[22] Similarly, one of the stated purposes of Methodist groups is "to watch over one another in love."[23] Think about twelve-step groups like Alcoholics Anonymous and how they "watch over one another," especially in regard to the dependencies they're striving to overcome.

Going to church on Sunday is one thing. Allowing a Christian fellowship to shape our lives as Christians is quite another matter. **A deeper Christian faith will inevitably mean finding a small community that can**

21. As discussed in the first chapter, the word "fear" does not have to denote terror, but can mean "out of reverence for Christ."

22. It is a phrase that has been utilized consistently to express the nurturing role of a Baptist congregation. An Internet web search for the expression "watch over one another in brotherly love" with "Baptist church" produces hundreds of hits.

23. The Methodist "General Rules" (1743), originally issued under the name of John Wesley and later including the name of his brother Charles, stated that a Methodist Society was "a company of men, 'having the form, and seeking the power of godliness,' united in order to pray together, to receive the word of exhortation, and to watch over one another in love, that they may help each other to work out their salvation"; in Wesley and Wesley, *Methodist Societies*, 69.

encourage our faithfulness, including our spiritual practices. If you're not part of a small group like this, try to find a Christian community that can help you in this way. If you are part of a small group, like a Sunday School class, you might ask how the group could better function to hold you and others accountable for our Christian practices.

Another way to be accountable for one's faithfulness is **spiritual direction,** a process by which a believer makes herself or himself accountable to a particular person, a **spiritual director** who can guide them individually along the path of self-giving love. A spiritual director will inquire carefully about the spiritual life of the one they direct and may prescribe particular exercises designed to move the person forward in their Christian journey, for example, particular forms of prayer or meditation appropriate to their particular needs.

The Christian journey is a journey towards self-giving love. In this journey **we need others, and others need us**. We help each other, we look out for each other, we watch over each other.

CHAPTER 7

The Goal of Self-Giving Love

I WANT TO INVITE you to a deeper Christian faith. The common thread that runs through the previous chapters is our belief in God's self-giving love (chapter 1), expressed in the Christian gospel (chapter 2). It is this belief that we profess as we become Christians (chapter 3), and it is this belief we celebrate in the Lord's Supper (chapter 4). The Christian community puts the stamp of self-giving love on its members by forming them after Christ at particular moments in life (chapter 5), and in the path of holiness by which people become saints in spite of themselves by God's grace (chapter 6). **Where is all this headed? What is its goal?**

If you're thinking maybe this is all headed somewhere in the direction of self-giving love, you're on track. But when we look beyond the present time to the future, we have to deal once again with more **language problems**. Our languages are really good at describing concrete, everyday things, the kind of stuff we live with from day to day. When we need to talk about something less familiar, like brain surgery or rocket science, we develop specialized vocabularies. When we talk about God and about God's future, as we will in this chapter, it takes more than specialized vocabularies. It takes something more like poetry, something that is never as precise or as verifiable or as falsifiable as we might like, but which is able to convey the powerful vision that **God's self-giving love will eventually triumph over all the horrors that have tried to thwart it**.

Maybe this is why **traditional Christian creeds and confessions of faith say so little about God's future and use cryptic language when they do speak about it**. The Apostles' Creed affirms our faith in "the resurrection of the body, and the life everlasting." The word translated "body" here means "flesh" or "meat," making very clear the commitment to a bodily resurrection. The Nicene Creed affirms that Christ's "kingdom will have no end," and it also affirms that "We look forward to a resurrection of the dead and life in the age to come."[1]

The Reign of God

As the Nicene Creed states, Christians live in the hope of Christ's coming reign or kingdom. Jesus taught us to pray,

ελθετω η βαcιλεια coy
γενηθητω το θελημα coy
ωc εν ογρανω και επι γηc

MAY YOUR REIGN COME
MAY YOUR WILL BE DONE
AS IN HEAVEN SO ALSO ON EARTH

Matthew 6:10

A monarch's reign is where the monarch's will is accomplished. Jesus spoke consistently about **the coming "reign" or "kingdom of God," the sphere in which God reigns, where God's will is done**. There's a problem with the traditional translation and punctuation of this passage, "Thy kingdom come, thy will be done, on earth as it is in heaven." That makes it sound like we're praying for God's will to be accomplished in heaven as well as on earth. The way it appears in the text of Matthew, however, it looks like God's will already *is* done in heaven, and we're praying that it be done *on earth* just as it *is* in heaven. We're also praying that God's reign would come *on earth*, just as it *is* already present in heaven.

I know there are some folks who say that God's reign can't come on earth because the earth is too screwed up for that to happen. Sometimes when I read the news feeds, it really looks that way. But what about God? Our hope for God's future is grounded in our faith in God's ability to bring about God's plan for the creation. Meanwhile, historic Christian communities are going to keep praying that God's reign will come upon the earth.

---

1. The Apostles' Creed and the Nicene Creed are cited from Pelikan and Hotchkiss, *Creeds and Confessions*, 1:669 and 1:163.

And not just praying; we're going to work by God's grace to make that a reality. Praying that God's reign will come on the earth is just about the same thing as praying that God's good will should prevail on the earth. God's will is done wherever God reigns.

I hear that some people are "so heavenly minded that they're no earthly good." People who are truly heavenly-minded can't abide the earth as it is. They've had a sight of better things, and their vision of the reign of God gives them a fiery, passionate desire to see things on earth change. Mother Teresa of Kolkata (Calcutta) was a heavenly minded woman. You want to tell me she did no earthly good? Martin Luther King Jr. was a heavenly minded man. Read or listen to his sermons, then tell me he was up to "no earthly good." Francis of Assisi, heavenly minded. William Wilberforce, heavenly minded. Thomas Merton, heavenly minded. Let's see: who accomplished good stuff on earth? **Give a little credit to the ones who have seen a vision of better things. Better yet, come join us.**

Will We Get What We Ask For?

If we have a vision of a better world where God's will is accomplished, **we also have reason to fear what might happen if God's will is not accomplished**. Let me restate that. We have reason to fear what's happening right now, when God's will is not being accomplished. One reason to fear God's justice is because we might get what we ask for. There's going to be hell to pay for some of the crap going on here. I've imagined showing up for the great judgment, and finding a sign that says:

NOTICE
PEOPLE FROM PLANETS
WHERE CHILDREN STARVE
ARE HEREBY CONSIGNED TO HELL FOREVER
NO WE DO NOT INTEND TO LISTEN
TO YOUR EXCUSES
GO TO HELL

Perfectly just. And then the ground opens up underneath us and we descend into the fires of Gehenna, never to return. That's what I'm afraid of: getting just what we ask for. If you think that's not biblical, please read Matthew 25:31–46. Read it literally, in the King James Version if you wish.

Really, **are we just asking for hell**, letting the world go on as it is?

ΤΟΤΕ ΕΡΕΙ ΚΑΙ ΤΟΙC ΕΞ ΕΥΩΝΥΜΩΝ
ΠΟΡΕΥΕCΘΕ ΑΠ ΕΜΟΥ ΚΑΤΗΡΑΜΕΝΟΙ
ΕΙC ΤΟ ΠΥΡ ΤΟ ΑΙΩΝΙΟΝ
ΤΟ ΗΤΟΙΜΑCΜΕΝΟΝ ΤΩ ΔΙΑΒΟΛΩ
ΚΑΙ ΤΟΙC ΑΓΓΕΛΟΙC ΑΥΤΟΥ

THEN HE WILL SAY TO THOSE ON HIS LEFT
GO AWAY FROM ME DAMNED ONES
INTO THE ETERNAL FIRE
PREPARED FOR THE DEVIL
AND HIS ANGELS

Matthew 25:41

Whatever happened to "Gentle Jesus, meek and mild"?[2] Or all that stuff about how the God of the Old Testament is a God of wrath and judgment and the God of the New Testament is a God of love and mercy?

Well here's what happened, according to Matthew 25, and it doesn't take calculus to figure this out. Jesus was a stranger; we didn't welcome him. Is that clear? Jesus was naked; we didn't clothe him. Need further explanation? Jesus was sick and in prison; we didn't visit him. Any questions, class? And then the stinger: "Truly I tell you, just as you did not do it to one of the least of these, you did not do it to me" (Matt 25:45). Need someone to paint a picture for you? Well, here it is.

The Bible uses a variety of imagery to describe eternal punishment: "the eternal fire prepared for the devil and his angels" (Matt 25:41), the image of the worm and the fire that destroy bodies after death (Mark 9:42–48), the image of separating the wheat and the chaff (Matt 3:12), the image of separating silver and dross (Prov 25:4, Isa 1:22).

Not all of these biblical images depict the final judgment as conscious, eternal torment, despite a strong Christian folk tradition that does depict God's judgment in that hellacious way. Some are images of immediate destruction. Christian communities have differed over whether hell means conscious eternal punishment or the annihilation of all that is contrary to God.

What Christian communities do agree on is that hell means separation from God. *The Catechism of the Catholic Church* (1992) states, "The

---

2. The words, "Gentle Jesus, meek and mild," are the beginning words of a hymn by Charles Wesley that first appeared in his *Hymns and Sacred Poems* (1742).

chief punishment of hell is eternal separation from God, in whom alone man can possess the life and happiness for which he was created and for which he longs."[3] Striking a very similar tone, evangelist Billy Graham said in a 1993 *Time* magazine interview, "The only thing I could say for sure is that hell means separation from God . . . When it comes to a literal fire, I don't preach it because I'm not sure about it."[4]

One popular notion about God's judgment is to believe that in the end God will save everyone. We should not doubt that God *wants* to save everyone, for God "desires everyone to be saved and to come to the knowledge of the truth" (1 Tim 2:4). But this view, universalism, implies that in the end we will not have the choice of separating ourselves from God, and it's difficult to square that with the biblical message because love cannot be coerced. Most Christian communities have rejected the teaching of universalism because it implies that in the end God will somehow coerce everyone into fellowship with God, whether they really want it or not. It might be better to say that **in the end we're going to get what we ask for**. If we want fellowship with Christ and with Christ's saints, we get that. If we don't want fellowship with Christ and with Christ's saints, well guess what? We just might get what we want.

"The fear of יהוה is the beginning of wisdom" (Prov 9:10a). We should fear God's judgment. I know there are people who are tormented and frozen by fear, and that's not healthy. If you have that kind of destructive fear, I hope you can find the help you need to overcome it. But **fear is an appropriate emotion**. Go ahead and be afraid. In the end, the matter of God's judgment comes down to whether we desire fellowship with God. If we don't want fellowship with God, we're not likely to follow his commandments, and if we don't desire fellowship with God, God's coming will be a terrible judgment. If we don't want fellowship with God, one way or another we're not likely to be happy about God's presence, now or later.

Those who love Jesus Christ and want to be in fellowship with him will return his self-giving love to others. This is why they will feed the hungry, clothe the naked, and visit the sick and those in prison, because in every person in need, they see the image of the Savior. **Judgment begins right now. Grace is available. Start by asking for grace.**

3. *The Catechism of the Catholic Church* (1994), para. 1035; in the English translation of Catholic Church, *Catechism of the Catholic Church*, 270.

4. Billy Graham, interviewed by Gibbs and Ostling, "God's Billy Pulpit," 70; see also Wacker, *America's Pastor*, 50.

Heaven as Self-Giving Love

If we love Jesus Christ, we will rejoice in his presence, now and when he comes again. If hell means eternal separation from God and from God's people, then **heaven means eternal fellowship with God and with God's people, and that also begins now**. A poet expressed it like this,

> In Christ, your head, you then shall know,
> shall feel your sins forgiven;
> anticipate your heaven below,
> and own that love is heaven.[5]

Just how God's future will work out for us remains a mystery, as the first letter of John explained:

ΑΓΑΠΗΤΟΙ ΝΥΝ ΤΕΚΝΑ ΘΕΟΥ ΕϹΜΕΝ
ΚΑΙ ΟΥΠϢ ΕϕΑΝΕΡϢΘΗ ΤΙ ΕϹΟΜΕΘΑ
ΟΙΔΑΜΕΝ ΟΤΙ ΕΑΝ ϕΑΝΕΡϢΘΗ
ΟΜΟΙΟΙ ΑΥΤϢ ΕϹΟΜΕΘΑ
ΟΤΙ ΟΨΟΜΕΘΑ ΑΥΤΟΝ ΚΑΘϢϹ ΕϹΤΙΝ

BELOVED WE ARE NOW CHILDREN OF GOD
AND IT HAS NOT APPEARED WHAT WE WILL BE
WE KNOW THAT WHEN HE APPEARS
WE WILL BE LIKE HIM
BECAUSE WE WILL SEE HIM AS HE IS

1 John 3:2

The passage explains something we do not know and something we do know about the future in Christ. **We do not know "what we will be."** Just as Paul struggled in 1 Corinthians to explain that our bodies are buried as material bodies and are raised as "spiritual bodies" (1 Cor 15:44), the author here professes that there is a mystery to what we will be like in the future reign of God. But there is one thing he professes to know: when Christ appears again, "we will be like him, because we will see him as he is."

How will we be like Christ? Perhaps the author is suggesting that our resurrection bodies will somehow be like the resurrection body of Jesus. But more importantly, I believe, **we will be like him because we will have**

5. Charles Wesley's poem, "For the Anniversary Day of One's Conversion," cited from United Methodist Church, *United Methodist Hymnal*, 57–58.

given ourselves up, we will have poured ourselves out in love, as Christ did (1 John 3:16). We do not need to worry about the mechanics of the resurrection. We need to focus on being Christlike. Judgment begins now. Grace is available. Start by asking. **The Christian life is a life in which we begin to live into the reign of God.**

Between Death and the Final Judgment

I have said that we don't need to worry about the mechanics of the resurrection, but one question inevitably comes up. **What happens between the time a person dies and the final judgment?** First Thessalonians 4:13 refers to Christians who have died as "fallen asleep." That suggests that between death and the final judgment, a person is unaware of the passage of time. You die, and the next instant you wake up to face the judgment. Martin Luther favored this view.[6]

The story of the rich man and Lazarus in Luke 16:19–31 suggests a conscious state between death and the final judgment. The story goes like this. Two men died, and after death they see each other, the poor man in "Abraham's bosom," and the rich man in "hades." If that sounds like the poor man went to heaven and the rich man went to hell, here's the problem. The rich man stated that he had five brothers whom he wanted to be warned about the coming judgment. If the brothers were still alive and could be warned about the judgment, then this had to be prior to the final judgment of the living and the dead, and, so the interpretation goes, it must denote a conscious state between death and the final judgment.

The Protestant reformer John Calvin, Anglican bishop John Pearson, and Methodist founder John Wesley believed in such an "intermediate state," as did many other Protestants, though they were unwilling to speculate about the precise nature of this state.[7] **The Catholic teaching about purgatory** is a particular version of teaching about such an intermediate state. Neither Calvin nor Wesley nor the Catholic Church believed that souls who had rejected Christ could somehow be justified or "saved" after

---

6. An example in Luther's work appears in his *Notes on Ecclesiastes* 9:5–6, in *D. Martin Luthers Werke: Kritische Gesamtausgabe*, 20:160–61; English language translation in Luther, *Luther's Works*, 15:147–48.

7. The teaching appears in Calvin's *Institutes* 3.25.6, in Calvin, *Calvin: Institutes*, 2:997–98. Two (out of many) examples from John Wesley's works are a) sermon "Dives and Lazarus" 1.3–5, in Wesley, *Sermons*, 4:7–8; b) sermon "On the Discoveries of Faith" ¶ 8, in Wesley, *Sermons*, 4:32–33.

death. The Catholic way of stating this is to say that purgatory is the porch of heaven—that is, it is only for believers, not a state or place where unbelievers could change their minds.[8]

Because of the wide differences in views on this subject, it's not really possible to state a consensus between Christian communities on this issue. It is important to know that there are biblical grounds for the various views that have been taken of the state between death and the final judgment. It may be that, as in many places where we speak about God and about God's future, our language and our concepts fail, and we're doomed to misunderstanding if we try to take biblical passages quite literally in cases like this. God has some surprises in store for us.

But there's one point that we should state as a common ground between Christian communities. **We believe that those who have died in the faith are in Christ, and that through Christ we continue to share fellowship with them,** whether they're "asleep" or awake "in the bosom of Abraham." The letter to the Hebrews speaks of this in a remarkable way. After giving a long list of Jewish and Christian saints who had maintained their faith in spite of adversity, the letter has this phrase,

ΤΟΙΓΑΡΟΥΝ ΚΑΙ ΗΜΕΙϹ
ΤΟϹΟΥΤΟΝ ΕΧΟΝΤΕϹ ΠΕΡΙΚΕΙΜΕΝΟΝ ΗΜΙΝ
ΝΕΦΟϹ ΜΑΡΤΥΡΩΝ

THEREFORE HAVING
SUCH A CLOUD OF WITNESSES
SURROUNDING US

Hebrews 12:1

There's a dramatic shift in this verse from the past tense that the letter had used to describe all the saints in chapter 11, to the present tense in this phrase, "Therefore having such a cloud of witnesses surrounding us." We don't know how, but **somehow those who share fellowship with Christ now surround us and give us strength to believe, even in the face of adversity.**

In the Apostles' Creed, traditional Western Christian communities confess their faith in **"the communion"** or fellowship **"of saints."** That

8. Catholic Church, *Catechism of the Catholic Church*, ¶ 1030–32 (in American translation, pp. 268–69).

doesn't just mean superstar saints. It means ordinary folks who kept the faith, who gave themselves, who reflected (however dimly) the beauty and the holiness of God. I'd guess it includes folks who never imagined they'd be numbered in "the communion of saints." But God accomplishes what we're not able to accomplish. Grace is available. Just ask.

Omega

Our language and our concepts fail, but **they point toward the horizon**. Look at the Greek alphabet chart at the end of this book, and you'll see that the first letter in the Greek alphabet is ﾒ, *alpha*, and the last letter in the Greek alphabet is ⲱ, *omega*. Here's something from the very end of the Christian Bible, from the book called *Apokalypsis* or Revelation:

ⲉⲅⲱ ⲧⲟ ⲁⲗⲫⲁ ⲕⲁⲓ ⲧⲟ ⲱ

ⲟ ⲡⲣⲱⲧⲟⲥ ⲕⲁⲓ ⲟ ⲉⲥⲭⲁⲧⲟⲥ

ⲏ ⲁⲣⲭⲏ ⲕⲁⲓ ⲧⲟ ⲧⲉⲗⲟⲥ

I AM THE ALPHA AND THE OMEGA

THE FIRST AND THE LAST

THE BEGINNING AND THE END

Revelation 22:13

At the omega-point on the horizon, everything comes together: good deeds, good thoughts, good poetry, good history, good music, good memories, good water, good wine, and good bread. They overshadow all the mediocre stuff that came before them. They finally crowd out all the horrors that went before them. Julia Ward Howe wrote during the Civil War in the United States,

> He is coming like the glory of the morning on the wave,
> he is wisdom to the mighty, he is honor to the brave;
> so the world shall be his footstool,
> and the soul of wrong his slave.[9]

The world itself is finally healed and consoled: "He will wipe every tear from their eyes" (Rev 21:4).

---

9. In United Methodist Church, *United Methodist Hymnal*, 717.

The world ends not with a bang and not with a whimper, but with a feast: the great marriage feast of "the Lamb slain from the foundation of the world." And the reign of God is finally realized as the revelers sing "like the sound of many waters,"

ΑΛΛΗΛΟΥΙΑ
ΟΤΙ ΕΒΑϹΙΛΕΥϹΕΝ ΚΥΡΙΟϹ Ο ΘΕΟϹ
Ο ΠΑΝΤΟΚΡΑΤΩΡ

ALLELUIA
FOR THE LORD GOD
THE ALMIGHTY REIGNS

Revelation 19:6

The world begins and ends with the self-giving love of God. The life we live as Christians today is a living into this vision of the coming triumph of self-giving love. Whenever we celebrate the Lord's Supper, we proclaim Christ's death "until he comes" (1 Cor 11:26), and we pray that the offering of ourselves will be one with his self-offering. Grace is available. Sometimes it tastes like bread and wine. Open your heart and your mouth and receive the grace given for you.

ΕΡΧΟΥ ΚΥΡΙΕ ΙΗϹΟΥ
Η ΧΑΡΙϹ ΤΟΥ ΚΥΡΙΟΥ ΙΗϹΟΥ
ΜΕΤΑ ΠΑΝΤΩΝ

COME LORD JESUS
MAY THE GRACE OF THE LORD JESUS
BE WITH ALL

Revelation 22:20–21[10]

---

10. *The Greek New Testament*, edited by Dirk Jongkind et al., has "with the saints," as some of the most ancient manuscripts have. Others of the most ancient manuscripts simply have "with all," and I'm inclined to think of "the saints" as an expansion of the meaning of the sentence.

Common Texts

Texts of the Lord's Prayer, the Apostles' Creed, the Nicene Creed, and the Summary of the Ten Commandments

THE TEXTS GIVEN HERE are the translations for the Lord's Prayer, the Apostles' Creed, and the Nicene Creed, as well as the summary of the Ten Commandments, and are given as they appear in the 1979 *Book of Common Prayer* of the Episcopal Church in the USA. For the sake of ecumenical usage, the doxology ("For thine is the kingdom . . ." etc.) is deleted from the Lord's Prayer, as is the *filioque* ("and the Son") clause in the Nicene Creed, with appropriate notes.[1]

---

1. The Lord's Prayer is given as it appears in the Episcopal Church, *Book of Common Prayer*, 97 (omitting the doxology); the Apostles' Creed is on page 96, and the Nicene Creed on pages 358–59 (omitting the *filioque* clause). The Summary of the Commandments (the Decalogue) is given on page 350.

The Lord's Prayer

Traditional English:

Our Father, who art in heaven,
hallowed be thy Name,
thy kingdom come,
thy will be done,
on earth as it is in heaven.

Give us this day our daily bread.

And forgive us our trespasses,
as we forgive those
who trespass against us.

And lead us not into temptation,
but deliver us from evil.[2]

Amen.

---

2. Many Protestant communities add at this point the doxology, in traditional English, "For thine is the kingdom, and the power, and the glory, for ever and ever."

Contemporary English:

Our Father in heaven,
hallowed be your Name,
your kingdom come,
your will be done,
on earth as in heaven.

Give us today our daily bread.

Forgive us our sins
as we forgive those
who sin against us.

Save us from the time of trial,
and deliver us from evil.[3]

Amen.

---

3. The doxology added by Protestants in contemporary English is "For the kingdom, the power, and the glory are yours, now and forever."

The Apostles' Creed

I believe in God, the Father almighty,
creator of heaven and earth.

I believe in Jesus Christ, his only Son, our Lord.
He was conceived by the power of the Holy Spirit
and born of the Virgin Mary.
He suffered under Pontius Pilate,
was crucified, died, and was buried.
He descended to the dead.
On the third day he rose again.
He ascended into heaven,
and is seated at the right hand of the Father.
He will come again to judge the living and the dead.

I believe in the Holy Spirit,
the holy catholic church,
the communion of saints,
the forgiveness of sins,
the resurrection of the body,
and the life everlasting. Amen.

The Nicene (Nicene-Constantinopolitan) Creed

We believe in one God,
the Father, the Almighty,
maker of heaven and earth,
of all that is, seen and unseen.

We believe in one Lord, Jesus Christ,
the only Son of God,
eternally begotten of the Father,
God from God, Light from Light,
true God from true God,
begotten, not made,
of one Being with the Father.
Through him all things were made.
For us and for our salvation
he came down from heaven:
by the power of the Holy Spirit
he became incarnate from the Virgin Mary,
and was made man.
For our sake he was crucified under Pontius Pilate;
he suffered death and was buried.
On the third day he rose again
in accordance with the Scriptures;
he ascended into heaven
and is seated at the right hand of the Father.
He will come again in glory
to judge the living and the dead,
and his kingdom will have no end.

We believe in the Holy Spirit, the Lord, the giver of life,
who proceeds from the Father.[4]
With the Father and the Son
he is worshiped and glorified.

4. Western churches traditionally add at this point "and the Son" (*filioque*).

He has spoken through the Prophets.
We believe in one holy catholic and apostolic church.
We acknowledge one baptism for the forgiveness of sins.
We look for the resurrection of the dead,
and the life of the world to come. Amen.

A Summary of the Ten Commandments

Hear the commandments of God to his people:

I. I am the Lord your God who brought you out of bondage.
You shall have no other gods but me.
Amen. Lord have mercy.

II. You shall not make for yourself any idol.
Amen. Lord have mercy.

III. You shall not invoke with malice the Name of the Lord your God.
Amen. Lord have mercy.

IV. Remember the Sabbath day and keep it holy.
Amen. Lord have mercy.

V. Honor your father and your mother.
Amen. Lord have mercy.

VI. You shall not commit murder.
Amen. Lord have mercy.

VII. You shall not commit adultery.
Amen. Lord have mercy.

VIII. You shall not steal.
Amen. Lord have mercy.

IX. You shall not be a false witness.
Amen. Lord have mercy.

X. You shall not covet anything that belongs to your neighbor.
Amen. Lord have mercy.

The Greek Alphabet

ⲁ	alpha
ⲃ	beta
ⲅ	gamma
ⲇ	delta
ⲉ	epsilon
ⲍ	zeta
ⲏ	eta
ⲑ	theta
ⲓ	iota
ⲕ	kappa
ⲗ	lambda
ⲙ	mu
ⲛ	nu
ⲝ	xi
ⲟ	omicron
ⲡ	pi
ⲣ	rho
ⲥ	sigma
ⲧ	tau
ⲩ	upsilon
ⲫ	phi
ⲭ	chi
ⲯ	psi
ⲱ	omega

Bibliography

Ali, Abdullah Yusuf, trans. *The Qurʾān: A Translation*. 19th US ed. Elmhurst, NY: Tahrike Tarsile Qurʾān, 2007.

The Apostolic Tradition. In *Hippolyte de Rome: La Tradition Apostolique d'après les anciennes Versions*, edited by Bernard Botte. Sources chrétiennes 11. Paris: Éditions du Cerf, 1968.

Aquinas, Thomas. *Summa Theologiae*. In *S. Thomae Aquinatis Summa Theologiae*, edited by Petrus Caramello. 3 vols. Rome: Marietta, 1952–1956.

Augustine. *Confessions*. Translated by R. S. Pine-Coffin. London: Penguin, 1961.

————. *Les Confessions*. Edited by Aimé Solignac. Bibliothèque Augustinienne: Œuvres de Saint Augustin 13–14. Paris: Desclée de Brouwer, 1962.

Ayoub, Mahmoud M. *Islam: Faith and History*. Oxford: Oneworld, 2004.

Barth, Karl. *Dogmatics in Outline*. San Francisco: Harper & Row, 1959.

Benedict of Nursia. *The Rule of St. Benedict*. Edited and translated by Bruce L. Venarde. Dumbarton Oaks Medieval Library. Cambridge, MA: Harvard University Press, 2011.

Bettenson, Henry, ed. *Documents of the Christian Church*. 2nd ed. Oxford: Oxford University Press, 1963.

Bilezikian, Gilbert. *Christianity 101*. Grand Rapids, MI: Zondervan, 1993.

Blume, Clemens, ed. *Sequentiae Ineditae: Liturgische Prosen des Mittelalters*. Analecta Hymnica Medii Aevi series. Leipzig: O. R. Reisland, 1900.

Boswell, John. *Christianity, Social Toleration, and Homosexuality: Gay People in Western Europe from the beginning of the Christian Era to the Fourteenth Century*. Chicago: University of Chicago Press, 1980.

————. *Same-Sex Unions in Premodern Europe*. New York: Villard, 1994.

Botte, Bernard, ed. *Hippolyte de Rome: La Tradition Apostolique d'après les anciennes Versions*. Sources chrétiennes 11. Paris: Éditions du Cerf, 1968.

Bradshaw, Paul F. *Reconstructing Early Christian Worship*. Collegeville, MN: Pueblo Books / Liturgical Press, 2010.

Calvin, John. *Calvin: Institutes of the Christian Religion*. Translated by Lewis Ford Battles and edited by John T. McNeill. 2 vols. Library of Christian Classics 20–21. Philadelphia: Westminster, 1960.

Campbell, Ted A. *The Gospel in Christian Traditions*. New York: Oxford University Press, 2009.

Catholic Church. *The Catechism of the Catholic Church*. Washington, DC: United States Catholic Conference, 1994.

Bibliography

―――. "Directory for the Application of Principles and Norms on Ecumenism." http://www.vatican.va/roman_curia/pontifical_councils/chrstuni/documents/rc_pc_chrstuni_doc_25031993_principles-and-norms-on-ecumenism_en.html.

―――. *The Sacramentary: Approved for Use in the Dioceses of the United States of America by the National Conference of Catholic Bishops and Confirmed by the Apostolic See.* Collegeville, MN: Liturgical, 1984.

Church of England. *Certain Sermons or Homilies Appointed to be Read in Churches in the Time of Queen Elizabeth of Famous Memory.* London: Society for Promoting Christian Knowledge, 1890.

Cummings, Brian, ed. *The Book of Common Prayer: The Texts of 1549, 1559, and 1662.* Oxford: Oxford University Press, 2011.

Dib, Pierre. *History of the Maronite Church.* Translated by Seely Beggiani. Detroit: Maronite Apostolic Exarchate, 1971.

Edgerton, Franklin, trans. *The Bhagavad Gītā.* Cambridge, MA: Harvard University Press, 1944.

Ehrman, Bart D. *Lost Christianities: The Battles for Scripture and the Faiths We Never Knew.* Oxford: Oxford University Press, 2003.

Enchiridion Biblicum: Documenta Ecclesiastica Sacram Scripturam Spectantia. 4th ed. Naples: D'Auria, 1961.

The Episcopal Church. *The Book of Common Prayer.* New York: Oxford University Press, 1979.

Fiorenza, Elisabeth Schüssler. "Missionaries, Apostles, Coworkers: Romans 16 and the Reconstruction of Women's Early Christian History." *Word & World* 6.4 (1986) 420–33.

Furnish, Victor Paul. *The Moral Teaching of Paul.* 3rd ed. Nashville: Abingdon, 2009.

Gibbs, Nancy, and Richard N. Ostling. "God's Billy Pulpit." *Time* 142 (1993) 70–78.

Gihr, Nicholas. *The Holy Sacrifice of the Mass: Dogmatically, Liturgically, and Ascetically Explained.* New York: Herder, 1943.

Grahame, Kenneth. *The Annotated Wind in the Willows.* Edited by Annie Gauger. New York: Norton, 2009.

Gros, Jeffrey, et al., eds. *Growth in Agreement II: Reports and Agreed Statements of Ecumenical Conversations on a World Level, 1982–1998.* Geneva: WCC, 2000.

Harkness, Georgia. *What Christians Believe.* Nashville: Abingdon, 1965.

Hays, Richard B. *The Moral Vision of the New Testament: Community, Cross, New Creation.* San Francisco: HarperSanFrancisco, 1996.

Heitzenrater, Richard P. *Wesley and the People Called Methodists.* 2nd ed. Nashville: Abingdon, 2013.

Heppe, Heinrich. *Reformed Dogmatics: Set Out and Illustrated from the Sources.* Translated by G. T. Thomson and edited by Ernst Bizer. London: Allen & Unwin, 1950.

Holmes, Michael W., ed and trans. *The Apostolic Fathers: Greek Texts and English Translations.* 3rd ed. Grand Rapids: Baker Academic, 2007.

Hopkins, Thomas J. *The Hindu Religious Tradition.* The Religious Life of Man. North Sciutate, MA: Duxbury, 1971.

Hordern, William. *A Layman's Guide to Protestant Theology.* New York: Macmillan, 1955.

Hurtado, Larry W. *Lord Jesus Christ: Devotion to Jesus in Earliest Christianity.* Grand Rapids, MI: Eerdmans, 2003.

Bibliography

Ishak, Fayek M., trans. *A Complete Translation of the Coptic Orthodox Mass and the Liturgy of St. Basil.* Toronto: Coptic Orthodox Church, Diocese of North America, 1973.

James, William. *The Varieties of Religious Experience: A Study in Human Nature.* New York: Modern Library, 1902.

The Joint Commission of Churches in Turkey. *Christianity: Fundamental Teachings.* Istanbul: Turkish Bible Society, 2017.

Jongkind, Dirk, et al., eds. *The Greek New Testament.* Cambridge, UK: Cambridge University Press, 2017.

Julian of Norwich. *Revelations of Divine Love.* Translated and with an introduction by Clifton Wolters. Harmondsworth, UK: Penguin, 1966.

Justin Martyr. *Apologies.* In *Justin, Philosopher and Martyr: Apologies,* edited by Denis Minns and Paul Parvis. Oxford Early Christian Texts. Oxford: Oxford University Press, 2009.

Kittel, Gerhard, and Gerhard Friedrich, eds. *Theological Dictionary of the New Testament.* Translated and edited by Geoffrey W. Bromiley. Grand Rapids, MI: Eerdmans, 1964.

Kittel, Rudolf, ed. *Biblia Hebraica* [*Biblia Hebraica Stuttgartensia*]. 4th ed. Stuttgart: Württembergische Bibelanstalt, 1977.

Kittel, Rudolf, et al., eds. *Biblia Hebraica Stuttgartensia.* 16th ed. Stuttgart: Württembergische Bibelanstalt, 1973.

Knowles, David. *The Evolution of Medieval Thought.* New York: Vintage, 1962.

Lewis, C. S. *Mere Christianity.* New York: MacMillan, 1960.

Luther, Martin. *The Babylonian Captivity of the Church.* Translated by A. T. W. Steinhäuser. In *Three Treatises,* 113–260. 2nd rev. ed. Minneapolis: Fortress, 1970.

———. *Notes on Ecclesiastes; Lectures on the Song of Solomon; Treatise on the Last Words of David.* Vol. 15 of *Luther's Works,* edited by Jaroslav Pelikan. 55 vols. Saint Louis: Concordia, 1972.

———. *Three Treatises.* 2nd rev. ed. Minneapolis: Fortress, 1970.

Lutheran-Roman Catholic Dialogue. "Joint Declaration on the Doctrine of Justification." In *Creeds and Confessions of Faith in the Christian Tradition: Statements of Faith in Modern Christianity,* edited by Jaroslav Pelikan and Valerie Hotchkiss, 3:877–88. New Haven: Yale University Press, 2003.

MacDonald, Gary Bruce. "By Faith By Hope." *Journal of the Clan Campbell Society of North America* 42.2 (2015) 16–17.

McKinnon, James, ed. *Music in Early Christian Literature.* Cambridge Readings in the Literature of Music. Cambridge, UK: Cambridge University Press, 1987.

———. *The Temple, the Church Fathers, and Early Western Chant.* Aldershot, UK: Ashgate, 1998.

McLuhan, Marshall. *The Gutenberg Galaxy: The Making of Typographic Man.* Toronto: University of Toronto Press, 1962.

Minns, Denis, and Paul Parvis, eds. *Justin, Philosopher and Martyr: Apologies.* Oxford Early Christian Texts. Oxford: Oxford University Press, 2009.

Mommsen, Theodor, ed. *Chronica Minora Saec. IV. V. VI. VII.* Monumenta Germaniae Historica 9. Berlin: Weidmann, 1892.

Morin, Jean. *Commentarius de Sacris Ecclesiae Ordinationibus Secundum Antiquos Et Recentiores Latinos, Græcos, Syros Et Babylonios . . .* Rev. ed. Rome: Barbiellini, 1758.

Mynors, R. A. B. *C. Plini Caecili: Epistularum Libri Decem.* Oxford: Clarendon, 1963.

Bibliography

Neusner, Jacob, et al. *Do Jews, Christians, and Muslims Worship the Same God?* Nashville: Abingdon, 2012.

Oden, Thomas C. *Agenda for Theology.* San Francisco: HarperCollins, 1979.

Otto, Rudolph. *The Idea of the Holy: An Inquiry into the Non-Rational Factor in the Idea of the Divine and its Relation to the Rational.* Translated by John W. Harvey. 3rd rev. ed. Oxford: Oxford University Press, 1926.

Pelikan, Jaroslav. *The Christian Tradition: A History of the Development of Doctrine.* 5 vols. Chicago: University of Chicago Press, 1971–89.

———. *Credo: Historical and Theological Guide to Creeds and Confessions of Faith in the Christian Tradition.* New Haven: Yale University Press, 2003.

Pelikan, Jaroslav, and Valerie Hotchkiss, eds. *Creeds and Confessions of Faith in the Christian Tradition.* 3 vols. New Haven: Yale University Press, 2003.

Peters, F. E. *The Harvest of Hellenism.* New York: Simon & Schuster, 1970.

Pliny the Younger. *Letters.* In *C. Plini Caecili: Epistularum Libri Decem,* edited by R. A. B. Mynors. Oxford: Clarendon, 1963.

Ratzinger, Joseph [Pope Benedict XVI]. *Introduction to Christianity.* Translated by J. R. Foster. New York: Herder & Herder, 1970.

Sanders, E. P. *Jewish and Christian Self-Definition.* 3 vols. Philadelphia: Fortress, 1980.

Schmid, Heinrich. *The Doctrinal Theology of the Evangelical Lutheran Church.* Translated by Charles A. Hay and Henry E. Jacobs. 3rd rev. ed. Minneapolis: Augsburg, 1899.

Schoedel, William R. *Ignatius of Antioch: A Commentary on the Letters of Ignatius of Antioch.* Edited by Helmut Koester. Hermeneia—A Critical and Historical Commentary on the Bible. Philadelphia: Fortress, 1985.

Stead, Christopher. *Divine Substance.* Oxford: Clarendon, 1977.

Sumney, Jerry L. *Steward of God's Mysteries: Paul and Early Church Tradition.* Grand Rapids, MI: Eerdmans, 2017.

Tanner, Norman P., ed. *Decrees of the Ecumenical Councils.* 2 vols. London: Sheed & Ward, 1990.

Tappert, Theodore G., trans. and ed. *The Book of Concord: The Confessions of the Evangelical Lutheran Church.* Philadelphia: Fortress, 1959.

Tertullian. *De Ieiunio [On Fasting].* In *Corpus Christianorum Series Latina,* 2:1255–77. Turnhout, Belgium: Brepols, 1954.

Thayer, Joseph Henry, trans. *Thayer's Greek-English Lexicon of the New Testament: Being Grimm's Wilke's Clavis Novi Testamenti, Translated, Revised, and Enlarged.* New York: American Book Company, 1889.

Theissen, Gerd, and Annette Merz. *The Historical Jesus: A Comprehensive Guide.* Translated by John Bowden. London: SCM Press, 1998.

United Methodist Church. *The Book of Discipline of The United Methodist Church 2012.* Nashville: United Methodist, 2012.

———. *The United Methodist Hymnal: Book of United Methodist Worship.* Nashville: United Methodist, 1989.

Vööbus, Arthur, trans. *The Didascalia Apostolorum in Syriac.* Corpus scriptorum Ecclesiasticorum orentalium. 2 vols. Louvain: Secrétariat du CorpusSCO, 1979.

Wacker, Grant. *America's Pastor: Billy Graham and the Shaping of a Nation.* Cambridge, MA: Harvard University Press, 2014.

Ware, Timothy Kallistos. *The Orthodox Church.* Harmondsworth, UK: Penguin, 1964.

Wesley, Charles. *Hymns for Those that Seek, and Those that Have Redemption in the Blood of Jesus Christ.* Bristol: Farley, 1747.

Bibliography

Wesley, John. *Sermons*. Edited by Albert C. Outler. 4 vols. Bicentennial Edition of the Works of John Wesley. Nashville: Abingdon, 1984–87.

Wesley, John, and Charles Wesley. "The General Rules of the United Societies." In *The Methodist Societies: History, Nature, and Design*, edited by Rupert Davies, 9:67–75. Bicentennial Edition of the Works of John Wesley 9. Nashville: Abingdon, 1989.

———. *Hymns and Sacred Poems*. Bristol: Farley, 1739.

———. *Hymns and Sacred Poems*. Bristol: Farley, 1742.

———. *The Methodist Societies: History, Nature, and Design*. Edited by Rupert Davies. Bicentennial Edition of the Works of John Wesley 9. Nashville: Abingdon, 1989.

———. *A Wesley Reader: Writings of John and Charles Wesley*. Edited by Ted A. Campbell. Dallas: Tuckapaw Media, 2008.

Wildman, Wesley J. *Religious and Spiritual Experiences*. Cambridge: Cambridge University Press, 2011.

Wilken, Robert L. "The Christians as the Romans (and Greeks) Saw Them." In *Jewish and Christian Self-Definition*, edited by E. P. Sanders, 1:111–13. Philadelphia: Fortress, 1980.

World Council of Churches Faith and Order Commission. *Baptism, Eucharist and Ministry*. Faith and Order Paper no. 111. Geneva: WCC, 1982.

———. *Confessing the One Faith: An Ecumenical Explication of the Apostolic Faith as it is Confessed in the Nicene-Constantinopolitan Creed (381)*. Faith and Order Paper no. 153. Geneva: WCC, 1991.

Young, Frances. *Sacrifice and the Death of Christ*. London: SPCK, 1975.

———. *Virtuoso Theology*. Cleveland, OH: Pilgrim, 1993.

Zagano, Phyllis. *Holy Saturday: An Argument for the Restoration of the Female Diaconate in the Catholic Church*. New York: Herder & Herder, 2000.

Glossary and Index

Items in **boldface** have brief definitions or explanations; items in regular (not bold) type are simply index references. The abbreviation "q.v." means "which see"; that is, it refers readers to a different entry in this glossary and index. The abbreviations "n." and "nn." (plural) refer to references in footnotes.

Absolution: Pronouncement of forgiveness on the part of a Christian community, 75–76

Acclamation of the Gospel: Liturgical proclamation of the death and resurrection of **Jesus Christ**, 22–24

Accountability: See **Discipline**.

AD: In small capital letters, a traditional and specifically Christian designation, *Anno Domini*, "The Year of the Lord."

Adonai: Hebrew, "Lord," a word traditionally pronounced in place of the unpronounced **Name of God** in Jewish piety and practice, 3, 99

Adult Baptism: See **Baptism**

Advent: The initial season of the Christian **Liturgical Year** that begins on the fourth Sunday before Christmas and celebrates the prophecies of the coming (advent) of **Jesus Christ**, 35

Agape: See Love and **Love Feast**.

Agnosticism: Doubt, especially about the **Existence of God**, 11

Allāh: Common Arabic noun for "God" used by Christians, Jews, and Muslims, also used as a **Name of God** in **Islam**, 3–4

Amen: Hebrew, "So may it be"; typically used to conclude a prayer, 23, 30, 68–69

Anabaptist Churches: Churches that originated in the period of the reformations, characterized by their practice of believers' baptism, 50

Anglican Churches: Churches that trace their spiritual and liturgical traditions as well as their church polity to the Church of England, which became formally distinct from the Catholic Church at the time of the reformations (1500s), 47, 56 n. 1, 102, 105

Anointing: Application of oil for healing or cleansing, 26, 39, 50, 52, 53, 73–74, 82, 86–87, 91–92

Glossary and Index

Anointing of the sick: A special form of anointing for persons who are seriously ill, accompanying prayers for healing; the expression has been used in the Catholic Church since 1973 to describe the sacrament that was until that time referred to as "last rites" or "extreme unction.", 86–87

Apolutrosis: New Testament Greek term (Rom 3:24–25) often translated "redemption"; the process by which a person was released or redeemed from captivity by payment of a ransom (*lutron*), 61

Apocrypha *or* Deuterocanonical writings: Writings included in the canon of Christian scriptures by the Catholic Church and some Eastern Christian churches that did not exist in Hebrew at the time of the reformations and for this reason were excluded from the canon of scripture received in Protestant churches, 19

The Apostles' Creed: A Western baptismal creed, sometimes also referred to as the old Roman baptismal creed. Although the received text of this creed dates from the 700s, earlier forms with nearly the same wording appeared from the 300s, 20–21, 43–44, 46, 47, 88, 102, 115–116, 122, 128

The Apostolic Tradition: An ancient document (ca. 200 ad) that describes Christian worship customs and church organization. Although sometimes attributed to Hippolytus of Rome, the authorship of the document is disputed, 45–47

Aquinas: see Thomas Aquinas

Arianism: The belief advocated by the presbyter Arius of Alexandria, ca. 320 AD, that maintained that Christ is a created being who does not share the full divinity of God the Father. The **First Council of Nicaea** and the **Nicene Creed** were directed against Arianism.

Assemblies of God: US-based denomination reflecting the teachings of Pentecostal churches, 112 n. 20

The Assyrian Church of the East: The separated Eastern Christian church that has refused to use the term ***Theotokos*** (q.v.) to describe the Blessed Virgin Mary and rejects the teachings of ecumenical councils after ad 381, 32, 33, 56 n. 1

Athanasius of Alexandria: Bishop of the church of Alexandria in the early 300s ad who defended the teachings of the Council of Nicaea and helped define the canon of Christian scriptures, 20

Atheism: Denial of the **Existence of God**; see also **Agnosticism**, 11

Augsburg Confession (1530): One of the principal and earliest confessions representing the doctrine of Lutheran churches, 31 n. 29, 32 n. 30, 67 n. 19, 79,

Augustine of Hippo: Ancient African theologian (354–430) who laid the foundations of Western Christian thought, 16, 45, 70 n. 27, 95–96

Ayoub, Mahmoud M, 4 n. 6, 28 n. 25, 101 n. 9, 110 n. 18

Baptism: The ritual use of water "in the name of the Father and of the Son and of the Holy Spirit" that brings a person into the Christian community, 37–54, 74

    Adult Baptism (baptism with profession of faith), 50, 54

    Baptismal Names, 50–51

    Believer's Baptism: see Adult Baptism (baptism with profession of faith)

    Immersion, 49–50

    Infant Baptism, 50–54, 90,

    Pouring, 49–50

    Rebaptism, 51

    Sprinkling, 50

Glossary and Index

Baptism of the Holy Spirit: The term designates a **religious experience** following conversion described by **Holiness Churches** as **Entire Sanctification** (q.v.) and by **Pentecostal Churches** as an empowerment by the Holy Spirit normatively accompanied by the initial evidence of speaking in unknown tongues, 48, 112

Baptist churches: Christian communities that originated in the 1600s holding a congregational form of church government and practicing believers' baptism, 50

Barth, Karl, xiii n. 7

Believer's Baptism: See **Baptism**.

Benedict of Nursia and Benedictine Monasticism: Benedict of Nursia (ca. 480–547 AD) was an influential leader of monastic houses whose *Rule* for the monastery at Monte Cassino became the pattern for Benedictine monasticism, 78–79, 105

Benedict XVI (Joseph Ratzinger), xiii n. 7

Bhakti: A **Hindu** term meaning "devotion.", 41–42

The Bible: The Christian Bible contains (at least) thirty-nine books of the Old Testament, twenty-seven books of the New Testament, and in some traditions, it includes other disputed books described as apocryphal or deuterocanonical, 19–20, 103–107

Bilezekian, Gilbert, xiii n. 7

Bishop: The office of an "overseer" or superintendent in historic Christian communities,

Bless, Blessing: To bless means "to make happy." It came to denote actions by which something or someone is made holy or sanctified, but continued to carry the meaning that a blessed person would be made happy, 88–89

Book of Common Prayer: Book containing the liturgies of **Anglican** Churches, derived from the *Book of Common Prayer* of the Church of England, 24 n. 20, 32 n. 31, 44, 47, 64 n. 15, 81 n. 8, 89, 99 n. 7, 102, 105, 125

Boswell, John, 81, 82 n. 9

Burial: Christians traditionally bury the bodies of believers, as a way of honoring the body, 87–89

Calvin, John: Protestant theologian (1509–1564) whose reforming work led to the existence of **Reformed Churches**, 44, 67, 121

Canon of Christian Scriptures: The list of writings received in Christian communities as authoritative scriptures, 19–20

Catechesis: The process of training and formation in the Christian faith, ix-x, xi, xiii, 38, 41, 42–47, 49, 52, 54 n. 18

Catechist: one who teaches **catechesis**, 43, 54 n. 18, 69

Catechumen: A person undergoing Christian training and formation (catechesis) in preparation for baptism, 69

Catholic: (a) The root meaning of the word is the Greek expression *kath' oles* (Acts 9:31), meaning "through the whole." The term has come to denote the universality of Christian churches throughout the inhabited world and the fullness of Christian teaching. (b) "The Catholic Church" as a title refers to those churches that are in communion with (share full fellowship with) the Bishop of Rome (the Pope). One of the twenty-two churches in communion with the Bishop of Rome, one is Roman Catholic in its church law, liturgy, and forms of spirituality, 23–24, 32–33, 46, 47, 50, 51, 52, 53, 56v n. 1, 66, 76, 79, 82, 105, 111–112, 118–119, 121–122

Celibacy: The term denotes the state of a person who makes a deliberate choice to remain single and thus not to marry. See also **Monks, Monasticism**, 77–79

Celibacy of Clergy, 79

Glossary and Index

Chant: See **Music**.

Chrismation: An anointing following baptism, considered to be one of the seven mysteries acknowledged by Eastern Orthodox churches. See also Confirmation, 53, 90–91

Christ: See Jesus Christ.

Christian Church (Disciples of Christ): US-based denomination derived from the Restorationist movement that separated from the **Churches of Christ** around the turn of the twentieth century.

Christian Initiation: A term designating the whole process by which persons come to faith in Christ and are incorporated into Christian communities, typically including personal faith (**conversion**), **catechesis**, **profession of the faith**, **baptism** (often with anointing), and **first communion**, 37–54

Christmas: The annual celebration (traditionally December 25, Christmas Day) of the birth of Christ and, more generally, the season ("Christmastide") from Christmas Day until **Epiphany** (January 6), 34–35

Church of the Nazarene: US-based denomination derived from the Wesleyan and **Methodist** tradition, the largest of **Holiness churches (q.v.)**:, 112 n. 19

Churches of Christ: US-based denomination derived from the Restorationist movement and which separated from the **Christian Church (Disciples of Christ)** around the turn of the twentieth century, xii, 56, 70–71

Collier, Charlie M, xi

Commandments: The central codes of behavior in the Bible; see also **Great Commandment** and **Ten Commandments**, 98–100

Communion: 1) Fellowship (q.v.); 2) a term ("Holy Communion") used by some Christian communities for the Lord's Supper, 55

The Communion of Saints: Belief expressed in the **Apostles' Creed** that Christians have **fellowship** or communion with all those, living and deceased, who have held the Christian faith.

Confession of Faith: Communal statement reflecting consensus on central beliefs; see also **Profession of Faith**, 123

Confession of Sin: Admission that we have sinned and need divine help (grace), 72–73, 75–77hes.

Confirmation: Profession of Faith usually simultaneous with Chrismation in Western Christian (**Catholic** and **Protestant**) churches, 41–43, 46–47, 52–54, 73, 90–92

Congregational Churches: Churches of the **Reformed tradition** characterized by a congregational form of church government, 52

Conversion: Turning to **Jesus Christ**, with **repentance for sin** and **faith** (trusting) in Christ, 38, 39–42, 111

The Coptic Orthodox Church of Egypt: Egyptian part of the family of **Oriental Orthodox Churches** that look to the Patriarch of Alexandria as the representative head of their church tradition, 22–23

Council of Chalcedon: Council of Christian bishops (431 AD) whose teaching on the one Person of Christ in two natures (divine and human) are received as an Ecumenical Council by Catholic, Eastern Orthodox, and some Protestant churches, 32–33

Council of Nicaea: See Nicene Creed (on the First Council of Nicaea)

Council of Trent: Catholic Council (1545–63) that codified the reforms of the Catholic Reformation, 44, 66 n. 18

Creation: The Christian Bible and historic creeds affirm that the material creation is God's good work.

Creed(s): From the Latin *credo*, "I believe." Statement(s) of essential elements of Christian faith on the part of a Christian community; see also **Confession of Faith**, 20–22, 115–116

Cremation: Many Christian communities have allowed for the cremation of the bodies of believers, especially since the 1960s, 89

Cross (image of): See also **Jesus Christ: Death** and **Sign of the Cross**.

Curse: Wishing evil on someone, as opposed to **blessing**, 15–16

Deacon, Deaconess: One ordained to serve (Greek *diakonein*) in Christian churches, 82, 84–85

Death and prayers for the dying, 86–87

Didache: an ancient Christian document thought to have been compiled in the mid-second century (100s AD), but which incorporates some material that may date from as early as the first century, 49, 50 n. 12

Discipline: Christian communities often hold members accountable for particular promises they have made, such as in monastic communities or in small groups for Christian discipleship, 43, 78, 112–114

Divine Liturgy: Term used to describe the Lord's Supper in Easter Orthodox churches, 55, 59, 91

Divorce: See **Marriage**.

Easter: The annual celebration of Christ's resurrection from the dead that falls (according to the formula of the **First Council of Nicaea**) on the first Sunday after the first full moon after the vernal equinox, 34–36, 109

Eastern [Christian] churches: A collective term generally denoting **Eastern Orthodox churches**, **Oriental Orthodox churches**, **Eastern-Rite Catholic churches**, and sometimes including the **Assyrian Church of the East** and the **Mar Thoma Church**, 32–33, 46, 52, 53, 79, 91, 111

Eastern Orthodox churches: Ancient Christian communities that accept all of the seven Ecumenical Councils (325–787) and share full communion or fellowship with each other, 32–33, 50, 51

Ecumenical Movement: Movement for visible unity of Christian communities that began early in the twentieth century.

Elder, presbyter, priest: An office of ordained ministry in historic Christian communities. Since the fourth century AD, elders have been authorized to preside at the Lord's Supper, 23, 70, 76, 79, 83–85, 86

Entire Sanctification: Methodist and **Holiness** churches teach that it is possible to love God completely (see **Great Commandment**) in this life by a gift of divine grace, 112

Epiphany (Theophany): Celebration of the Christ's revelation ("Theophany" in **Eastern Christian Churches**) to the gentile (non-Jewish) world. The Day of Epiphany is traditionally celebrated on January 6, and the season of Epiphany or Theophany extends from this date to the beginning of **Lent**, 34–35

Eternal (attribute of God), 10, 12, 13

Eucharist: Term used to describe the Lord's Supper in some historic Christian communities and in ecumenical circles, 55, 66, 69, 77, 91

Eulogy: Part of a traditional Christian **Funeral** or memorial service remembering and celebrating a deceased believer, 88

Glossary and Index

Evangelical:
> a) In a general sense, whatever has to do with the gospel (Greek *evangelion*); see **Gospel.**
> b) In a second sense, the term is sometimes used to distinguish Protestants (and specifically Lutherans) from Catholics; see Protestant churches.
> c) In a third sense, the term denotes Protestants who emphasize the unmediated authority of the Bible and the need for a personal experience of conversion, 53

Evangelical churches and communities: The term usually denotes churches that share the third sense of Evangelical given above, that is, churches that emphasize the unmediated authority of the Bible and the need for a personal experience of conversion, 41, 53

Evil: That which is opposed to the good intention of God; see also **Sin,** 47, 93–96

Excommunication: Separation from a Christian community or fellowship, 74–75

Existence of God, 11–12, 93

Experience: See **Religious experiences.**

Extempore Prayer: Prayer that is improvised at the moment as contrasted with memorized or written prayers, 102–103

Extreme Unction: See Anointing of the sick.

Faith: Belief; trusting in God. The term as a noun can also denote the content of Christian faith; i.e, "the faith.", 40–41

Fasting: Abstaining from food to heighten spiritual awareness, 8, 34, 56–57, 78, 83–84, 90, 107–110, 111

Fear of God: Appropriate awe and reverence for God. "Fear" in this sense is sometimes described as the fear of offending a loved one, 6–8, 10, 113, 117, 119

Feasting: Sharing food and drink together, which balances **Fasting** in Christian religious culture, 55–59, 62, 71, 77, 89–90, 110, 124

Fellowship: Sharing together; the New Testament Greek word for fellowship, *koinonia*, can also be translated "communion.", 29, 56, 57–59, 62–65, 67, 75, 77, 101, 119–122

Filioque Clause: The expression "and the Son" (Latin *filioque*) added to the Third Article of the Nicene Creed in the Catholic Church in the 700s AD, affirming that the Holy Spirit "proceeds from the Father and the Son.", 125, 129 n. 4

Fiorenza, Elisabeth Schüssler, 85 n. 16

First Communion: The first occasion when a person receives the Lord's Supper in a Christian community; part of the process of Christian Initiation, 37, 52–53

First Council of Nicaea: See Nicene Creed.

Forgiveness: Willingness to be reconciled to a person despite the ways in which they may have offended one, 18, 26, 73, 74–77, 92,

Francis of Assisi, xii, 117

Friends: The Society of Friends (also called Quakers) is a religious movement that originated in England in the 1640s, emphasizes the centrality of immediate experience of God, and does not practice the outward sacraments (i.e, baptism with water or the Lord's Supper with bread and wine), 38, 48

Funeral: Christian celebration of the life of a believer, often associated with burial or cremation, 88–89

Furnish, Victor Paul, 82 n. 9

Glossary and Index

God: Christian belief in God maintains monotheism characteristic of Judaism and Islam and the distinctive teaching that the one God is known in the three persons of the divine Trinity, 1–13, 14, 18–19, 24–34, 36, 38, 45–47, 57, 62–63, 72–75, 93–96, 97–100, 102–103, 111–112, 115–117, 118–120

Gospel: The "good news" (Greek *evangelion*) about Jesus Christ, expressed in a primitive formula in 1 Corinthians 15:1–4, 2, 14–36, 57–58, 64, 77, 108

Grace: God's power that enables people to do what they cannot do on their own, 91–92, 95, 96–98, 99–100, 103, 112, 115, 119, 124

Graham, Billy, 119

Grahame, Kenneth, 6–7

Great Prayer of Thanksgiving: See **Lord's Supper**.

Great Commandment(s): The commandment to love God with all one's being (Matt 22:35–38, Mark 12:28–30, Luke 10:27a; cf. Deuteronomy 6:4–5) and the related commandment to love one's neighbor as one's self (Matt 22:39–40, Mark 12:31, Luke 27b; cf. Lev 19:17–18), 44, 72–73, 99

Greek Orthodox Church: Part of the family of **Eastern Orthodox Churches** in communion with the Ecumenical Patriarch of Constantinople, historically utilizing Greek-language liturgy, 85

Guadalupe: See **Mary**: Virgin of Guadalupe.

Hands, laying on: Placing hands on a person's head, accompanied by prayers for their consecration or **ordination**.

Harkness, Georgia, **xiii n.** 7

Hays, Richard B, 82 n. 9

Healing: Wholeness of body and soul. See also **Anointing of the Sick**, 85–87

Heart: In the Bible, the "heart" denotes the center of the affections and often (as in the Hebrew *levav*) the mind or intellect as well.

Heaven: The ancient terms rendered as "heaven" generally denote the sky as opposed to the earth, though the term also denotes wherever God reigns; see also **Reign of God**, 120–121

Hebrew and Aramaic Scriptures: See **Old Testament**.

Heidelberg Catechism

Hell: Final separation from God, 117–119

Hinduism: Religious traditions indigenous to the Indian subcontinent that teach the way of release from the cycle of birth, death, and rebirth by way of ritual practice, performance of duties appropriate to one's caste and station in life, ascetic and meditative practice, and devotion (see *bhakti*), 41–42

Holiness Churches: Churches that arose in the United States in the late 1800s, carrying on the teaching of **John Wesley** about the possibility of **entire sanctification** in this life and usually insisting on a distinct religious experience of entire sanctification (sometimes called the **Baptism of the Holy Spirit** in Holiness churches, but not to be confused with the distinct Pentecostal meaning of this phrase), 85

Holy, Holiness: The term denotes that which is set aside or set apart for a religious purpose; in Christian cultures, the term "holiness" describes the nature of God.

The Holy Spirit: The Third Person of the divine **Trinity**.

Howe, Julia Ward, 123

Saint: A holy person, one who reflects God's holiness, x, 57, 67, 89, 95–96, 100, 103, 111, 112, 115, 119, 122–123, 124 n. 10

Saint's Day: A day to commemorate a particular saint. Traditionally martyrs and saints were celebrated on the date of their deaths, 89

Salvation Army: a Christian community derived from British Methodist churches that has emphasized social work among the urban poor and suspended the practices of baptism and the Lord's Supper, 48

Scriptures: see Bible.

Sermon, Preaching: The **New Testament** records early Christian announcement or preaching of the message of the gospel (e.g, Saint Peter's sermon in Acts 2) and early Christian services for the **Lord's Supper** included exhortations based on the reading of the **Bible**. Preaching was a central emphasis in the **reformations** of the 1500s, 14–15, 37, 38, 56, 69–70, 79, 88

Shahadah: The principal **Islamic** profession (confession of faith), 3–4

Shema: The Jewish affirmation beginning with Deut 6:4–9 that asserts the oneness of God and the call to love God with one's whole being, 2–3, 100

Shepherd **of Hermas**: An ancient Christian text from the second century (100s AD) that offers the possibility of **Repentance** for **Sin** committed after **Baptism**, 74

Sin: Any turning away from God, or anything that separates humans from God's good intention for them, 54, 61, 74–77, 93–96

Single Life: See **Celibacy**.

Sleep of the Soul: Teaching favored by **Martin Luther** and **Lutheran churches**, according to which the state of believers between death and the final judgment is a state of "sleep" or unconsciousness, 121–122

Small Groups: Christian communities have sometimes utilized small groups for discipline. Early Methodist class meetings and band meetings are examples of small groups for accountability, though many Pietistic groups have utilized such groups, sometimes called "conventicles.", 113–114

Spiritual Direction: The process of placing oneself under the direction of a spiritual adviser (spiritual director) who can help the believer discern and work on their own path to self-giving love, 114

Spiritual Gifts: Gifts (Greek *charismata*) of the Holy Spirit, such as those mentioned in 1 Corinthians 12 and 14, for the edification of Christian communities, 82–83.

Sprinkling: See **Baptism**.

Substance (divine): The **Nicene Creed** uses the term "substance" (Greek *ousia*) to describe God's being, and describes Christ as being "of the same substance" (Greek *omoousios*) with the Father, 29–30

Sunday: Early Christians met "on the first day of the week" (Acts 20:7), and the expression "the Lord's Day" (Rev 1:10) came to describe the Christian observance of Sunday as a Sabbath, 34, 52, 56, 57, 59, 68, 70, 110

Syriac Maronite Church of Antioch: An Eastern-rite church in communion with the Catholic Church, 85

Ten Commandments: The **Commandments** given to Moses as recorded in Exodus 20:1–17, and Deuteronomy 5:4–21. The numbering of the commandments differs in Christian communities, although the substance is the same, 44, 98–100, 131

Teresa of Kolkata (Calcutta, "Mother Teresa"), 117

Tertullian: Ancient North African Christian writer, ca. 200 AD, 59, 108

Theissen, Gerd, 16 n. 3, 27

Glossary and Index

Theophany: See **Epiphany.**

Theotokos: "the God-bearer," a term ascribed to the Blessed Virgin Mary by the Councils of Ephesus and Chalcedon, sometimes translated "Mother of God," contested by **Nestorius** and the Assyrian Church of the East, affirmed by other ancient churches (**Catholic,** Eastern **Orthodox,** and **Oriental Orthodox**) and by some Protestant churches, 31–33

Thomas Aquinas: Medieval European theologian (1225–1274) who clarified and defended Catholic beliefs, 11, 66

Torah: The first five books of the **Bible;** the heart of Jewish Scriptures, 19, 68, 98

Training in the Faith: See **Catechesis.**

Transubstantiation: A particular understanding of Christ's **presence** in the **Lord's Supper** favored in Catholic theology since the late Middle Ages, according to which the substance of bread and wine are entirely replaced by the substance of Christ's human body and blood, though the outward appearances of bread and wine remain, 66

Trinity: The worship of God as the three coeternal persons: the Father, the Son, and the Holy Spirit. See also **Persons of the Trinity, Substance (divine), Tritheism,** and **Modalism,** 28–30, 46, 48, 51

Tritheism: The belief rejected by traditional Christian communities that holds the Father, the Son and the Holy Spirit to be three Gods, 29

Turkey, Joint Commission of Churches in, xiii, 4 nn. 6–7, 11 n. 23, 5 n. 12, 11 n. 23, 22 n. 17, 41 n. 4, 51 n. 16, 60 n. 9, 94 n. 2, 99 n. 8

Twelve-Step (or Twelfth-Step) Movements, 8, 113

Universalism: The belief that all persons will be saved, 119

Via negationis ("the way of negation"): The "way of negation" is a spiritual practice by which the mystery of God is contemplated by negating (denying) terms that state the limitations of our experience, 10–11

Virgin of Guadalupe: The apparition of Saint Mary to **Juan Diego** in 1531 was in the form associated with apparitions of Mary in Guadalupe in Spain. The apparition to Juan Diego is understood as a blessing of Native American peoples and has become a sign of the **Catholic** identity of Mexico, 111–112

Vocation: The term literally means "calling," the sense of particular calling(s) that Christians have as a result of divine grace, 73–74, 82–85, 90

Ware, Timothy (Kallistos), 85 n. 17

Wesley, Charles (1707–1788): Poet and hymn writer who also led a branch of the Methodist movement, along with his brother John Wesley, x, xii, 89, 118 n. 2, 120

Wesley, John (1703–1791): Leader of the Methodist movement within the Church of England, 88, 98 n. 6, 102, 109, 112, 113 n. 23, 121

Westminster Shorter Catechism, 44

Wilberforce, William, 117

Wildman, Wesley J, 7 n. 16

Women: See **Ordination:** Ordination of Women.

World Council of Churches: A fellowship of Christian churches organized in 1948 as a result of the **Ecumenical Movement.** The following references are almost entirely from documents of the Council's Faith and Order Commission, xiii n. 6, 2 nn. 1–2, 4 n. 8, 6 n. 13, 14 n. 1, 24 n. 22, 29 n. 26, 31 n. 28, 38 n. 1, 40 n. 2, 45 n. 8, 49 n. 11, 50 n. 13, 53, 57 n. 2, 60 n. 8, 66 n. 16, 67 n. 22, 69 n. 25, 82 n. 11, 84 n. 15, 85 n. 19